PREFACE

It seems so long ago. And also, just like yesterday. ... ...
was an epidemiological event, Covid, especially in its lockdown
phase, was a social sounding. Life was heard differently. Streets
denuded of people and traffic; the wailing sirens of ambulances
ferrying the stricken to hospital ICUs; the drop-outs and tininess of
Zoom; the semi-spontaneous music ensembles as we leaned out of
our windows to clap, whoop and bang pots in support of frontline
workers; our heightened awareness of bird song and susurrating
breezes: all of it felt strange, new, consequential.

Whispers of mortality. A time of brooding and shivers. Lockdown
made us question whether we, as individuals or as a society, were
as ballasted as we had thought. How was it that we were united in
paeaning those nurses, cleaners and toilers whose voices were so
inaudible to us just weeks earlier? Those birds, that wind, rain: why
did they sound miraculous? In the Global North, music, mostly
in the form of data packets, is available on tap; yet the art and act
of actually listening – as opposed to merely hearing – is in decline.
More offers less. Music, particularly lossy digital music, has become a pollutant as baneful as microplastics or forever chemicals.

Artur Jaschke's *Mind The Music* is a learned, searching meditation
on the importance of listening. And of music. And of what sound
is - and can be. It does so, perhaps surprisingly, through sustained
attention to improvisation. Why surprisingly? Because improvisation – or improv – is often pilloried as naïve or feral, heady and
academically joyless, skronky noise, an inchoate and incoherent
racket, the preserve of socially maladapted men, an elitist private
language. Tellingly (and cheekily), Trevor Barre subtitles *Beyond
Jazz*, his enthusiastic chronicle of English improvised music between 1966 and 1972, "Plink, Plonk & Scratch".

Jaschke, who is a jazz player as well as a scientist, with his specialty in neuro-musicology, listens to improvisation differently. He hears it not only as music, but as a form of ethics. A space of engagement. He's of a mind with the great Victor Schonfield who, back in 1968, wrote, "Music is a chance for self-development. It's another little life, in which it's easier to develop the art of giving, an art which makes you more joyous the more you practice it. The thing that matters most in group music is the relationship between those taking part. The closer the relationship the greater the spiritual warmth it generates."

In *Mind The Music* too, improvisation is relational. And existential. It's a set of techniques that allows us to question conventions, capitalist realism, the status quo. It contributes, Jaschke believes, "to our understanding of the world around us and the ability to choose how we can interrupt this multisensory stimulus." Improvisation is not so much the sound of freedom as an unending commitment to freedom – a tense, enthralling negotiation between yesterday and tomorrow, the centripetal and the centrifugal, learning and unlearning, fear and hope. "That split-second moment between on and off, between alive and dead, is the moment of the actual act of improvisation." Who could fail to be compelled by this drama, this spelling out of the stakes involved?

Equally important, given the digital determinism of so many educators and politicians, their genuflection to algorithms and to the flawed theology of artificial and machine learning, is how much value Jaschke places on the relationship between improvisation and what he calls "embodied experience". I'm reminded here of musician Matt Davis who once told interviewers, "Listening is so much focused on space, that the piano extends to the whole space, to the room, to the air, and I feel as if I'm inhaling. It feels as if the act of listening and my body encompass the whole room, people, everything. It feels as if everything is inside me, that I'm in the room, that I'm vibrating with the space."

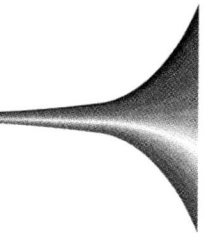

MIND THE MUSIC

ARTUR C. JASCHKE

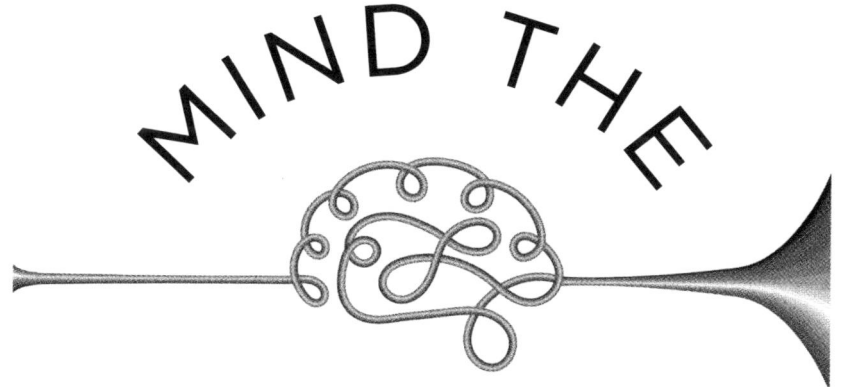

MIND THE
MUSIC

MUSIC,
IMPROVISATION AND
THE BRAIN

With a preface by Sukhdev Sandhu

The New Menard Press

TABLE OF CONTENTS

PART I:
WHAT IS IMPROVISATION?
(AND WHAT IS MUSIC?)

PART II:
MUSIC, IMPROVISATION
AND THE BRAIN

PART III:
THE SECRET OF IMPROVISATION

Mind The Music is expansive and ambitious. Some readers will respond most keenly to those sections in which Jaschke draws on his clinical expertise. Others will be more drawn to his references to John Coltrane and Godspeed You! Black Emperor. Sometimes, as when he describes the experience of listening to Miles Davis's remarkable *Bitches Brew* LP (1970), his brain scientist and his jazz performer selves are married: "You are trying to understand the musical event ... Our neurons are all firing, our networks are moving between the known and the unknown, and synapses are slowly searching for new points they can attach to, in order to learn how to handle this new stimulus."

By all means read this book to learn about improvisation and about the brain. Remember though, and Jaschke is very clear on this, improvisation is about something grander still: it "allows us to communicate and share, it can start revolutions ... courage and honesty are its constant companions."

Sukhdev Sandhu
New York, October 2023

AUTHOR'S NOTE

We are living in exceptional times. The consequences of the COVID-19 pandemic have caused great concern, and the measures taken to combat it have restricted our freedoms. Even though there were multiple economic and political initiatives to save some sectors, like the food and travel industries, we have to admit that in light of past crises it is the arts sector that has and will continue to suffer most retrenchments, years from now.

Over the past one hundred years, human beings have only once before experienced a pandemic on such a large scale, with the 1918 Spanish flu. Now that the World Health Organisation has announced that the Coronavirus is no longer a threat to humanity, we should be out of the woods—go back to normal and pretend that nothing ever happened. This, however, would be an illusion as the whole world was affected and it seems as if governments and policy makers have not yet learned their lesson, being unprepared for another pandemic on such a grand scale.

Each and every one of us had to live with measures to combat the virus. Some of these, i.e., working from home using technological innovations, have found their way into our everyday lives, post pandemic, where we embrace them as the 'new' normal. We cannot escape the fact that the pandemic has inevitably changed the way we see and experience the world we live in.

Even though science has repeatedly warned us of the possibility of such a global disaster, hardly any advice was taken seriously enough to increase funding for research. As we finally understand the importance of scientific research in times like these, its significance to society has shifted from an intriguing laboratory somewhat hidden on a university campus to the centre stage of global news.

Governments invested huge amounts of money into the search for a vaccine, having known for a long time that more structural funding and investment was needed to prepare for any crisis and especially one on such a scale. According to historian and professor Yuval Noah Harari in 2021, we might have just been paying the price for not having taken scientific research seriously enough.[1]

These days, hardly anyone will argue against the fact that we need to invest in many resources to prevent another large-scale disaster impact our lives again, as well as to ensure economic stability.

However, while listening to Godspeed You! Black Emperor's 'The Dead Flag Blues', we are slowly realising that this moment of potential *new normality*[2] marks the real danger post COVID-19.

As politics and the economy start to find ways to fill up the national coffers again, the work of care has only just begun. Long COVID, post-intensive care syndrome, post-traumatic stress syndrome, burnout, depression, fear, anxiety and social distancing as a new twenty-first-century virus will affect us all. Most of us will merely suffer from mild psychological discomfort and will be looking to distract ourselves with a good concert, a visit to the museum, an entertaining book, or a discussion about poetry. However, we will find ourselves falling into a gaping black hole. The cultural sector was hit hard during the crisis and will now be hit even harder, as there is a repeating pattern after every crisis: retrenchments in the arts and cultural sector, then in education, and finally in healthcare. While a more economic approach to the last two may be on hold for the near future—we have all seen the huge amount of work that has been done in the healthcare sector and experienced some form of home education and childcare—the arts and cultural sector will become the perfect victim, once again to be stripped to her bare bones and left shivering in the cold winds of the approaching cultural winter. Art will once again be considered a luxury item that does not contribute to anything substantial in world politics and economics, and which therefore can be cut in half, quarters and eighths, over and over again. But it is exactly the arts, with dance, fine arts, literature and music, which have to be at the new frontier of post-pandemic care.

We have all witnessed the balcony concerts in Italy, the communal singing from the windows of empty streets in Spain, musicians travelling to care homes and performing in front of the windows of the elderly, or healthcare staff simply listening to music while commuting home after an eighteen-hour shift in the intensive care unit. The arts allow us to reflect and express our feelings and have therefore become a part of our basic needs as human beings. Cutting the budgets in the cultural sector will halt the care that is needed now and will be needed for years to come. In moments of utter despair and crisis, many of us find our refuge and hope in the throbbing beat of a rhythm and blues song, the fast lyrics of a rap, the walking bass line of a jazz tune, the powerful sound of a rock song, the soothing strings of a symphony, or the loving memory of a warm safe place evoked by a ballad. Music resets our mind, allows us to escape the here and now for that one second. That second, which in neuroscientific terms is an eternity, allows our minds to touch base again, immerse ourselves in something greater than our thoughts, experiencing music with others at home, in a concert hall or at a festival. It is the music of all genres and in all its forms that like never before will bring people together. Music has generated hope and strength, that spark that makes us go the extra mile, sharing, expressing and experiencing our sorrows, pain, grief and fears, as well as our joys, laughter and jests.

The arts are essential to the development of every human being, starting before birth and accompanying us throughout our lives. It is the arts that make us human; knowing no boundaries or hierarchies, they allow us to bring these values into our interactions within society. In light of this, the digitalisation of music and advances in technology should not be fetishised but seen as an addition to the lives we live, the connections we make, the moments we share: we do not *store* memories, faces or interactions, we *story* them with and through the arts.

PRELUDE

The sound of brogues tapping on the asphalt. A lonely figure in a thick coat shields himself from the rain and biting wind. Pressing his hat against his forehead with his left hand, in his right hand he holds a black suitcase. As he walks underneath the streetlamps, they briefly light up his face. He doesn't look up or around and he almost disappears into the high collar of his coat. It is late, it is dark, the streets are empty. Lost in thought, he walks across the slippery sidewalk, step by step. Every now and then, a whistling sound—not a word—escapes from his lips.

The man looks up and is blinded by a bright light. He puts down his suitcase, places a hand to his eyes and tries, between his fingers, to locate the source of the light. The glare is becoming brighter and bigger—where is it coming from?

Suddenly, the light disappears. A police car passes by.

Slowly, his eyes adjust again to the dim light of the street lanterns, and around him the contours of the wet pavement are coming back, the little park bench beside him, the tall buildings, the neon signs and, in the distance, the Empire State Building. He reaches into his inside pocket for a cigarette and lights it with the greatest difficulty. "At the end of this street to the left ...," he mumbles.

Yes, there it is, the club where he is supposed to be. The man opens the door and is greeted by a curtain of heat and cigarette smoke. He puts his hat and coat on the coat rack. With his suitcase in hand, he walks to the back of the room.

"John, good to see you. We were afraid you got lost in this terrible weather," an agitated voice says.

John doesn't respond.

He walks past the club owner, places the saxophone to his lips, and the John Coltrane Quartet begins to fill the room with tones, rhythms, timbres and melodies.

With music.

––––––––––

This stereotypical image of a jazz musician probably resonates with you. Cigarette smoke, New York in the 1950s, bad weather, trilby hats … and musicians who bare their souls on stage. Improvisation in *optima forma*.

This is where we begin our journey into the fascinating network of connections in our brains that makes possible the phenomenon of *improvisation*, which is essential to our existence.

Essential?

Yes. Because no matter how much improvisation is associated with jazz music, the ability to improvise is certainly not reserved for jazz, and not even necessarily for music. Improvisation can be found in various styles of music and eras—from Hindustani music to Gregorian singing and the organ music of Johann Sebastian Bach.

But it is much more than that. It is also a means of communication, of solidarity, revolution, resistance.

EVERYONE CAN MAKE MUSIC

To get a sense of the wider understanding of improvisation used in this book, it might be useful to stay a little longer with the image I just sketched: the image of the creative jazz musician, someone who improvises within a musical context.

Music touches us and doesn't distinguish between people. Music connects us. Music is for everyone. And yet there are many people who say that, yes, they do enjoy listening to music, but to make it themselves, well, that's another thing entirely.

OH NO, THAT'S NOT FOR ME

But if you insist, the answer you often get is: *Sometimes I sing in the shower, but I would never sing in the company of others, and improvisation is truly beyond me.*

But nothing is further from the truth. Everyone can make music, everyone can improvise! We want to make music because we are surrounded by it. Music is everywhere. It would be tempting right now to cite a little green creature from a famous science-fiction tale: *It surrounds us and penetrates us; it binds the galaxy together.*

Okay, this might be taking it a little too far, but it is a fact that music is inextricably bound to our humanity, and that improvisation plays an important role in our lives.

Improvisation is courage: the courage to interpret a context anew, to verify new thoughts against reality, to let go of possible consequences. It is a dynamic process. And while all of us can do this—we really can—the internal mechanisms of music, and therefore of improvisation, remain incredibly complex.

Music is a world built from our experiences, our memories, our skills, our tastes—things that brain scientists have only recently begun to map due to the emergence of tools such as functional magnetic resonance imaging (fMRI) and diffusion tensor imaging (DTI).

HOW DOES MUSIC
TRIGGER OUR BRAIN?

Once we understand exactly how music functions in our brain and in our body, we can apply this knowledge to other, non-musical kinds of improvisation. Music is an incredibly intriguing phenomenon: the music we hear every day, on the car radio, on our earphones, in the supermarket, but also sounds that you would not immediately call music ... it all moves us—literally.

How does this work?

Let me, in this prelude, carefully begin to formulate an answer. Then, later in this book, we will go into greater depth.

Music is a succession of soundwaves that travel through the air until they touch our eardrums and cause them to vibrate. These mechanical vibrations are then transformed by the smallest bones in our body, the auditory ossicles, into electrical signals that our brain can interpret. Subsequently, these signals activate various areas in our brain, as well as several chemical substances—and this arrangement of signals, substances and connections in the brain makes it possible for us to create music.

Areas that deal with our emotions, that activate our memory, allowing us to plan, focus, listen, feel, look and perform an entire array of other tasks, all these areas play a role when we listen to music, when we play it, or when we improvise. In order to translate this large and complex brain activity into our behaviour and, thus, into the way we experience music—the way music touches us and moves us—we can distinguish four stages of musical participation: passive listening, active listening, playing music and improvisation. With each of these four stages, more brain areas are being activated, and with each step our brain is encouraged to challenge itself further, to work harder, and to grow.

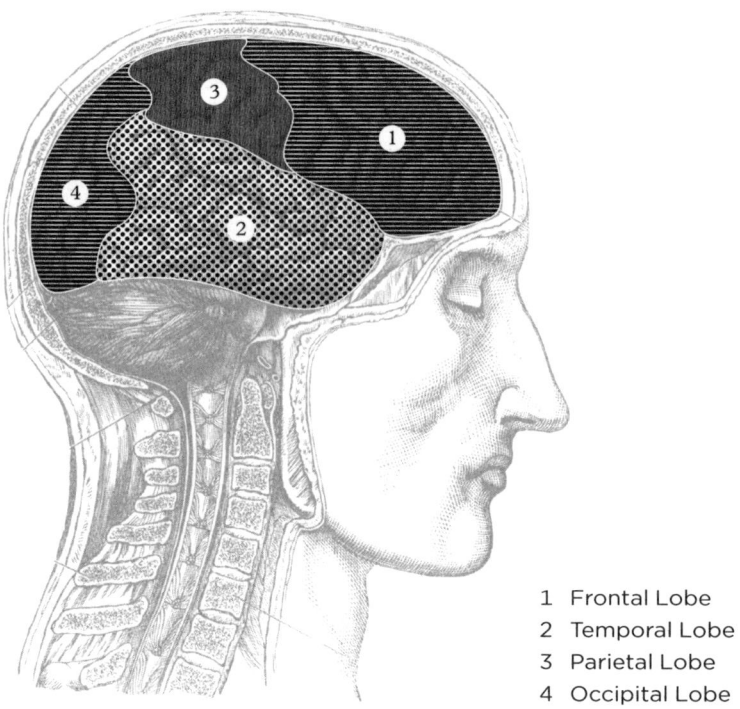

1 Frontal Lobe
2 Temporal Lobe
3 Parietal Lobe
4 Occipital Lobe

Notably, the fourth stage of musical participation, *improvisation*, is so much more than a number of brain areas talking to each other. Improvisation is inextricably bound up with the way we learn, the way we navigate the world, and the way we communicate.

You could almost say that it is in our DNA.

It is a fundamental part of our humanity and the way we engage with the world around us.

When we improvise, we don't look ahead; instead, we look back at our own cultural and historical luggage. This is something we can see and hear, for instance, in Scottish, Irish or Breton folk music, in the singing of Gregorian monks, or in the intriguing music of the Ottomans. We do not only use this cultural backpack when we improvise in a musical context, but also, and especially, during unexpected situations in our daily lives.

What we really mean when we say we're not good at improvising, *oh god, no* … is that we have *forgotten* how to do it.

We have forgotten how to be guided by our intuition.

By our ability to improvise.

EVERYBODY CAN IMPROVISE

Why, in a solo, do I play these notes and not others? Why do I also leave room for moments of silence? Why does improvisation come more easily to some than to others?

These are only a few of the questions that have preoccupied me since I have become both a neuroscientist and a musician. There are reasons why, in our research, together with my colleagues, I also focus on the relationship between music and the brain, on listening to music and making music, and on the ways in which we can implement this in our daily lives, as well as in education and in healthcare. How can we make use of music? Will it make us smarter? And why does music move us so deeply?

While searching for answers to these questions, I came across the phenomenon of improvisation. What is improvisation? How do talent and creativity work?

During research conducted in hospitals and nursing homes, and in the classroom with pre-schoolers and toddlers, we noticed that—in the words of cognitive music scientist and dear colleague Henkjan Honing—*everyone* has a sense of music. More so, even if some of the people in our research had never touched an instrument before, everyone was able to play something on a guitar, for instance, or on the piano, even together—the first musical improvisation of their lives. This came about not because they possessed a previously undiscovered hidden musical talent, but because the brain networks that are important for improvisation had already been created (in adults) or are still being created as a part of 'normal' development (in children) because we need them in our daily lives.

Humans can improvise—and secretly, we can do so exceptionally well—because it happens to be part of our creative heritage.

The only problem is that we don't realise this.

Do I see you shaking your head again?

I really cannot improvise, it's just not for me.

Let's take another example. It is raining cats and dogs and you are coming home with two large bags full of groceries. The handle of one of the bags is about to snap, your phone rings, you are soaked, and your neighbour is waving at you excitedly because he wants to discuss the latest political developments. You are not in the mood for this, so you start thinking of ways to avoid the situation—*I forgot to turn off the washing machine; I should really take this call; can we talk about this some other time?*

These are all mechanisms that require the skill to improvise.

You improvise your way out of an impending conversation.

Now maybe you will say that this an entirely different thing, totally unlike musical improvisation. But this is not the case. The areas of the brain that we use when we improvise with language are the same areas we use when we improvise musically. In fact, music activates many more additional brain networks, which makes it easier to improvise musically, because more brain areas collaborate to create improvisation.

It is obvious: all of us can do it, but we don't always have the courage to do so, or else we place an aesthetic label onto our improvisation: it isn't beautiful, it doesn't sound good.

We don't do the same with language because we have learned how to handle a vocabulary. We have remembered the things that work—and the things that don't.

We can do the same with music but, somehow, we just don't.

If everyone can do it, if we can all improvise, then why don't we let go of the labels *beautiful* and *ugly* and instead, just as with language, look for ways to make 'new' music?

This is where it gets complicated because who decides what is 'beautiful' or 'ugly'? Whether we like something depends mostly on our own tastes. But what is taste, and why do we prefer red instead of blue, or the other way around?

It is here that our personal development enters the picture, and the surroundings in which we grew up. From birth onwards we are being overwhelmed with stimuli, and they all shape us, whether it is the very first lullaby our parents sang to us, or the first pacifier with that cute little pink rag attached to it, or our favourite cuddly animal, the softest thing we ever touched. We store all these stimuli in our memory and they, subsequently, influence our tastes.

During puberty, we let go of all of this, and the things we loved until then are no longer 'cool'. We can even take an entirely different turn in our pursuit of ourselves, the world, and everything it holds. This is normal. It is precisely during puberty that the different areas in our brain are developing at various speeds. This means that one day we can be very empathetic, the next day we are suddenly terrible at planning, and yet another day we will find it difficult to regulate our emotions.

All these behavioural patterns are related to the kinds and the number of stimuli we received, and continue to receive, before and during puberty—and what we subsequently do with them. To put it differently, if everything was handed to us on a silver plate during this important developmental phase, if we would not be compelled to try to figure something out ourselves, to come up with an idea, to solve a problem instead of simply finding the answer online, then it would be very difficult for our brains to create new connections and grow stronger.

Perhaps you are thinking that this is the case only with teenagers, but nothing is further from the truth. It is precisely after puberty that all of us become lazy: we seek answers that are too obvious, and we avoid challenges in our search for ease and comfort. This tendency towards convenience hinders our brain development and will, in the long run, also affect our tastes and our insight into what we personally consider as 'beautiful' or 'less beautiful'.

HAS DIGITALISATION WEAKENED OUR MINDS?

We are increasingly losing the ability to make decisions based on what we (ourselves) have experienced and instead are becoming more and more distracted by loud external stimuli: every commercial that puts pressure on us to buy the newest model of mobile phone or laptop, every jingle that promotes a product, and every technological advancement that is supposed to make our lives so much easier. This has been happening since the 1930s—it is called *Neurolinguistic Programming* (NLP).[3]

If you continue this line of thought, you will see that ever since the 1930s we have been primed to mindlessly accept whatever kind of new gadget society presents to us, and to introduce them into our everyday lives without realising that these stimuli affect the things we like and why, how we relate to aesthetics, and what values we attach to them.

In a recent discussion about the use of different types of technologies, music and creativity, including *artificial intelligence* (AI), tech-writer Jacob Nelson awoke one morning with the not too unbelievable futuristic fantasy that one day we would be able to enter our smart kitchens where robots would make us coffee and fry an egg for us. In this future, we would be driven to work by smart cars while we relaxed behind the wheel and read a newspaper.[4]

Strangely, perhaps, this thought frightens rather than comforts me. No matter how wonderful this may sound, isn't it also the epitome of laziness and loss of independence? For example, scholarly research as we now know it would completely disappear. Instead of the many hours I used to spend in the library looking for essays and scholarly articles, today, this only takes me ten minutes thanks to a functional search engine such as Google.

In short, it appears that the effectiveness of the search engine has made us lazy. But doesn't this then create the time and space we need for creativity and the things we *really* want to do?

No, unfortunately it doesn't work like this. In the end it is all about finding a balance between having too many stimuli and having too few. If we are overwhelmed, we can no longer think clearly, and if nothing moves us, our minds will not be nourished; no new input also means no new output.

Imagine if suddenly you were to end up in the 1993 movie *Groundhog Day*. In this American movie from director Harold Ramis, you would be the grumpy weatherman who has been stationed in a small town against his will to report about a local superstition: waking up a groundhog to predict how much longer the winter will last. It is quite a spectacle and draws many people to town. But it wouldn't be a Hollywood movie if there weren't some kind of twist. And indeed, from that moment onwards, the protagonist wakes up every morning on the same day. In the beginning he fully enjoys the benefits of this loop in time. But after a while, boredom—and the desire to escape from this loop—drives him to extreme antics, including kidnapping the groundhog and driving himself, together with the animal, off a cliff. But even though he tries to end his life in this and various other ways, he continues to wake up the next morning on Groundhog Day.[5] I will not reveal here how the movie ends.

It might be extreme, but this example symbolises the increasing lack of input that results from the digitalisation of our lives. In other words, we allow our lives to be led by technology, we end up in an endless loop of predetermined input, and we lose our own capacity for innovative, creative ideas.

Is it really true that the digital era has weakened our minds? And has it perhaps forever prevented us from deep thinking?

In answer to this question, blogger Dominique Jackson writes mockingly that today's scouts need to learn how to use GPS-technology instead of a compass. Jackson argues that with every new technological invention, we become less active, both physically and cognitively, and that therefore we are becoming increasingly dependent on a screen, and he worries that one day we will become like those humans in the animation movie *Wall-E*, who spend their days lounging in chairs—the epitome of laziness.[6]

SOUNDS OF THE FUTURE

Such examples probably sound familiar to many of us. Perhaps we should ask ourselves whether or not we take technological developments too lightly, and in doing so, we lose ourselves more and more in the digital world, to such an extent that we leave almost anything up to a computer. We no longer truly challenge ourselves. Whether it is about a new pasta recipe, a cross-fit workout, a date, or a playlist on Spotify; in all these cases an AI or *machine learning* algorithm is used to offer you the best experience. Think, for instance, of the cookies in your browser. We leave behind a digital footprint, which is then picked up by an artificial intelligence that generates the kinds of commercials we would like to see. This is of course an interesting development, and we all use it to varying degrees—but still…

Let's stay with the example of commercials a little longer. And return to the most important themes of this book: music and improvisation.

How much of the music you hear in commercials is still being written by human composers? Or the music of the latest game you downloaded on your smartphone? Only one out of a thousand tunes are still being composed by a human being. And what about movie soundtracks? Yes, of course, people like Hans Zimmer and

Rachel Portman still exist, but a lot of the music you hear in movies is written by an AI.

Why?

To save money. Because artificial intelligence is becoming smarter, its potential in the creative industry, including music and music production, is also growing. Even if AI will not top the charts any day soon, algorithms are busy composing and performing music, and they even make money with their own compositions.

And why *would* we make music if an AI could do it for us?

If we create an algorithm that feeds an AI all the songs of The Beatles, this AI will write a song that sounds like The Beatles. But will it be innovative? Will this lead to new kinds of music? Would it not be more like a copy of what we humans would have also made—a matter of copy and paste?

Well, these are the sounds of the future, we could answer with a somewhat frivolous wordplay. *It is impossible to predict how it will be, but the computer will show us the way to the sounds of the future.*

But this, of course, is not how it works.

At this moment in time a computer is not yet able to play a creative, conscious and 'beautiful' improvisation. Such an improvisation will always be based on the input of the creative human brain, on the unique human skill to improvise. We should therefore not be looking into what a *machine* can do, but into how we *humans* improvise, how we can learn to improvise and how we can engage with it—and then maybe, one day, we can create something together with an AI.

But the most important thing—I have said it before—is that we already know how to do this, how to improvise, even if sometimes we think we don't. We have just forgotten how to, and, in some cases, we have even *unlearned* this skill. We should not let ourselves be distracted by technological developments, we should not lean back and relax and allow ourselves to be served by friendly robots or artificial intelligence. What distinguishes us from computers is precisely this: the fear, shame and uncertainty we feel when we improvise.

This is a book in praise of our marvellous ability to create something out of nothing—to improvise. The best way to sing this praise, I think, as a musician and a neuroscientist, is by 'simply' showing you how it works, improvisation. What we mean when we talk about it. What happens in our brains. And how these processes in our brains relate to our behaviour.

And so, we will continue the journey we started at the beginning of this prelude, with a visit to the John Coltrane Quartet.

Asking ourselves: how do we explain what happened there?

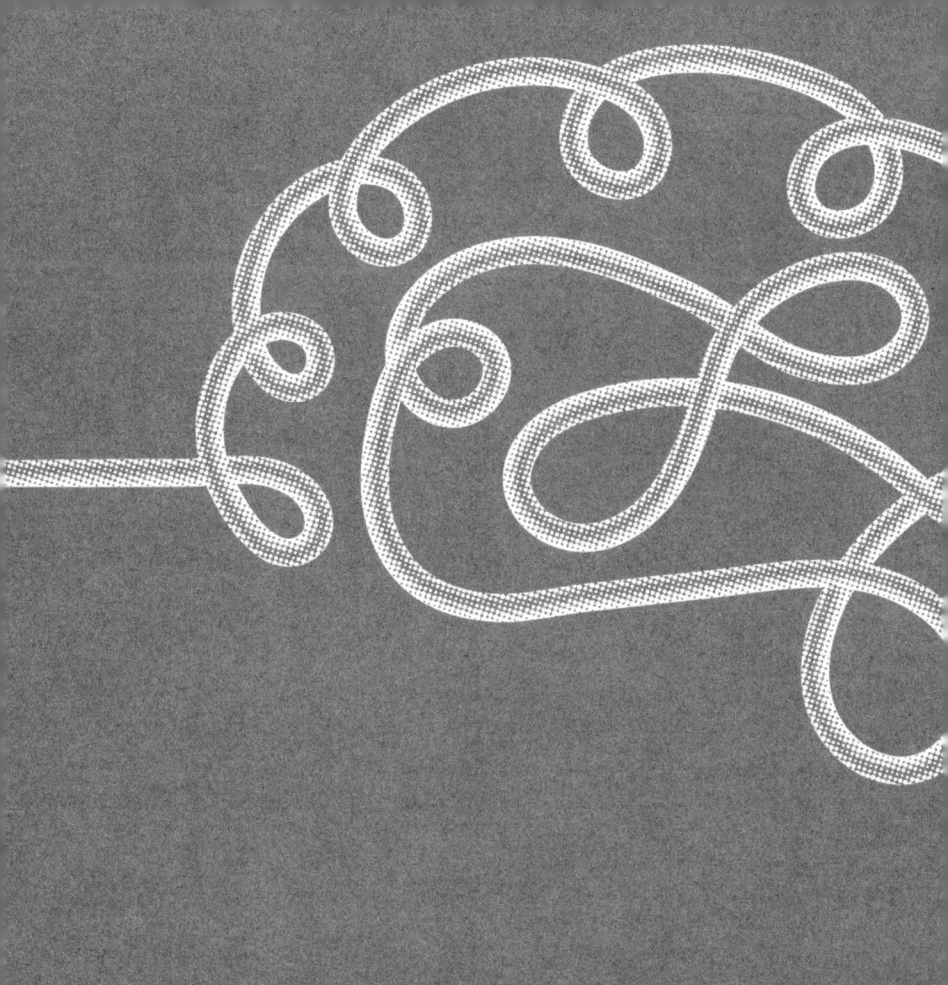

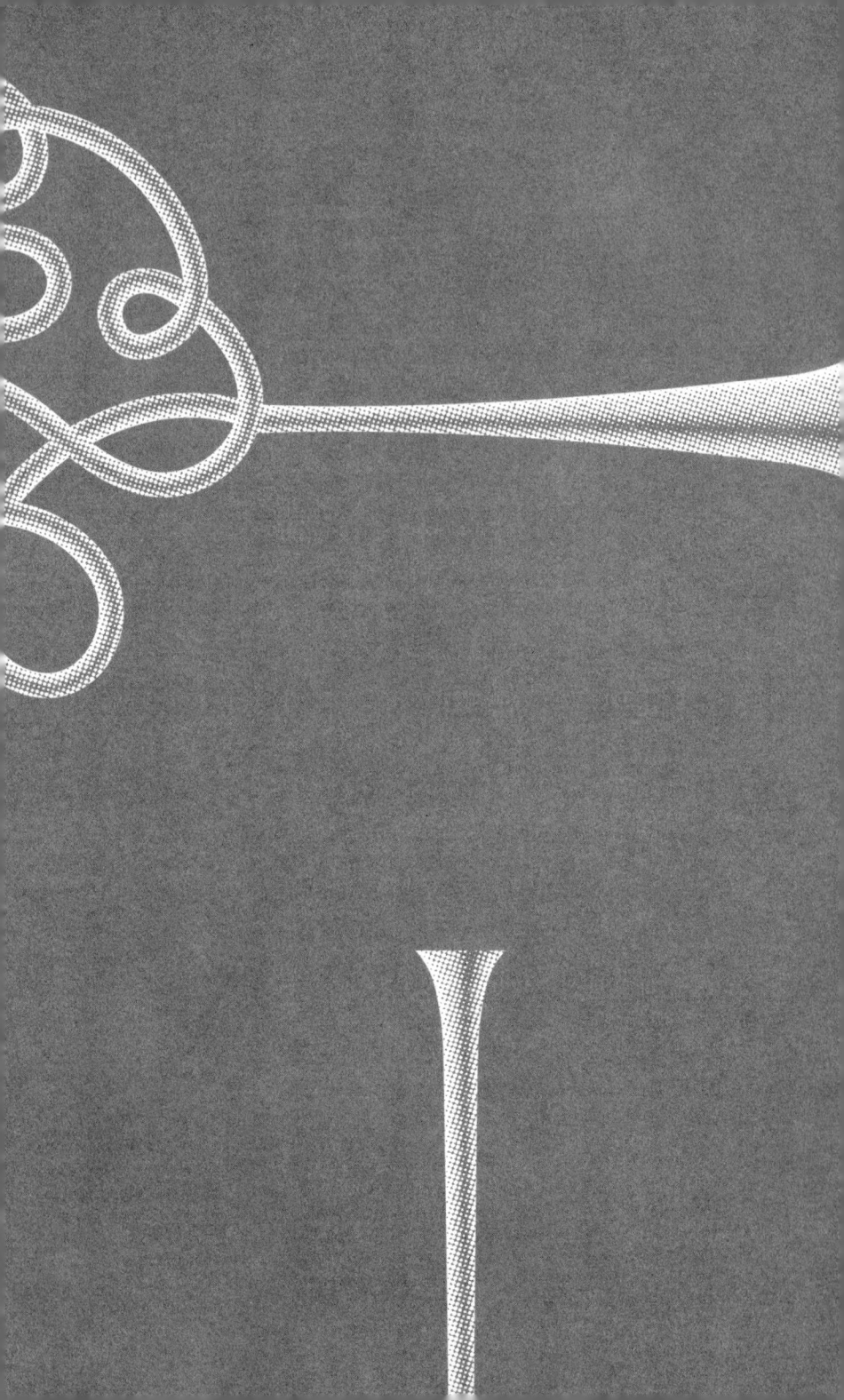

PART I

WHAT IS IMPROVISATION?
(AND WHAT IS MUSIC?)

1

A BRIEF HISTORY
OF THE EVOLUTION OF MUSIC

Humanity seems to be wedded to the idea that we listen to music as a pastime; something to accompany our ten-mile run in the morning or when preparing dinner. Even though music plays such an included role in our lives, we do not stand still even for a moment, asking ourselves what music really means to us, how we perceive it, and how it may affect our actions, such as running faster when hearing *Kind of Blue* by Miles Davis, or changing our ingredients to something more daring when Mahler's *Lieder eines Fahrenden Gesellen* suddenly blasts out of the speakers. As humans, we have the special quality of knowing what music to play to make ourselves feel even sadder, or when we are preparing for a party to put ourselves into a particular mood; we actively listen and choose the music.

Often, we do not choose the music ourselves, but leave the choice to the algorithm of the shuffle function of our music provider. We have reduced music to a readily accessible product that is there in the background, in our pockets, available at our fingertips at any given moment in time.

We do not always relegate music to the background but sometimes actively search for it in concert halls or community centres, with friends or family. This is something the 2020–21 pandemic has acutely brought home to us: think of the balcony concerts in Italy, or the street concerts in Spain, mentioned earlier. As humans we seek out the physical attributes of music, the feeling it creates, and the vibrations we experience when it flows through our body.

But what actually is music? Is it the sum of different sounds and rhythms that we all have agreed to appreciate and understand as music? Turning to the vast amount of scientific and non-scientific investigations on the subject, there is no clear answer to this question. On the one hand, we can argue that music is a product that has emerged from natural selection and, thus, is part of the evolution of the Homo sapiens. On the other, it can be seen as a random creation, which has found its way into our everyday lives without any further purpose. And yet it seems as if there must be more to music than evolution or uselessness when we are touched by socio-critical lyrics with a slightly ironical tone, enveloped in a catchy chorus line. Breaking music down into its components, it is indeed an accumulation of coordinated waves, forming frequencies in a harmonious or non-harmonious way, which reach our eardrum. From there, a mechanical signal—the movement of the eardrum to the frequencies—is translated into an electrical signal, which in turn can be interpreted by the brain with all its different networks and areas. So far there has been no emotion transmitted, no understanding of harmony or meaning[7], as Igor Stravinsky has famously observed. But already these coordinated sounds start to have an impact on our body, mind and behaviour. As we will learn later, individual sounds, like strumming one chord on a guitar, can already have a significant impact on the heart rate, blood pressure, stress genes and neural development in prematurely born infants.

Given the impact music can have on our state of being, investigations into our understanding of music have led us to agree that even the silent majority of music consumers who listen or dance to it, are musical. The diversity of cognitive and behavioural processes underlying such appreciation must therefore be rooted in human epigenetics, as it seems to be such a universal human trait. However, research on the genomics and bioinformatics of music is still scarce, even though it could help explain the biology and evolution of music and sounds at the molecular level. Genome-wide expressions could shed light onto human traits based on their molecular properties rather than anatomical regions. Most of the present genetic research is performed on either blood, saliva or stool samples, and rarely on brain samples, as these are not accessible in humans—at least not when looking at *in vivo* studies.

Based on gene-ontology analyses, or the analysis of biological function through our genes, research has focused on either the *up-regulation* or *down-regulation* of individual target genes, which in short is the process or reaction of genes to an external stimulus. Genes involved in up-regulation are associated with the transportation of neurotransmitters, such as dopamine, protein sumoylation and neuron protection. Neuroscientists Blood and Zatorre, in their ground-breaking study, have shown the importance of dopamine production when listening to music, analysing the human reward and motivation system together with brain regions associated with arousal, showing that when listening to and playing music our brains produce a vast amount of dopamine. Dopamine is one of the neurotransmitters involved when we are feeling very happy and aroused. Furthermore, these up-regulated target genes, which are related to music listening, are known to be associated with learning, memory and cognitive performance, song learning and singing in songbirds, auditory activation and absolute pitch, as well as neuroprotection, synaptic function (individual cell communication) and neurogenesis (the making of new brain cells). Conversely, down-regulation in genes is known to affect functions that are involved in the breakdown of cells, proteins and peptides and, moreover, related to the decay of brain cells, also known as neurodegeneration.

Nonetheless, listening to music has an overall positive impact as stress regulation genes are also affected, allowing for the reduction of stressors, impacting heart rate, blood pressure and oxygen levels, which in turn have a positive influence on our well-being.

2
THE HMMMM IN MUSIC

Given that music has such a profound effect on our genes and therefore on our development, it would appear that the appreciation of music, as well as playing it, has to be deeply rooted in humans. Music scientist Henkjan Honing has invested a great deal of his academic career into looking for the answer to the question whether music and musicality is something unique to humans.[8] His research has spanned decades of investigations and comparisons between human appreciation of music and how different animals perceive music, all in the quest to narrow the evolutionary gap between the different developmental stages of animals, from the Neanderthals to modern humans.

Ethnomusicologist John Blacking has searched within the observable human characteristics defined by our genes or phenotype in order to shed light onto the development of music. He approached the conundrum of music and musical appreciation from a single sound, which can be both musical and linguistic—the 'hmmmm'[9]. Blacking identified the hmmmm as a prelinguistic musical mode of thought and action, thus introducing a certain level of meaning to an expression. Blacking continued to use this expression to follow the different stages or lineages, in order to identify the possible development and embedment of music and musical thought in human evolution. Given the fact that our understanding of human biochemistry was very limited in the 1970s, Blacking nevertheless was able to conduct an extensive desk research of paleoethological and archaeological finds, together with ethnographic research, in different cultures across the world, to figure out how musicality as well as linguistics developed and shaped humanity. Understanding the expression of 'hmmmm' in this context, he introduced it into the lineage of the Homo ergaster who, with his advanced brain and anatomical adaptations for complex vocalisations, appears to be the first candidate in the long evolutionary line to the Homo sapiens sapiens. Ergaster, according to Blacking's research, used vocalisations from nearly two million years ago for foraging, mate competition and parenthood, as well as group activities, all of which can be registered and found in modern societies when looking at mothers or fathers singing to their babies just using humming sounds, also known as infant directed singing, which turns into infant directed speech. Blacking splits the development of this hm-mmmm sound into two developmental paths: the European Homo lineage and the African Homo lineage. The European lineage seems to be lost in translation more so than the African lineage, as an advanced hmmmm has seemingly not evolved further than in its meaning. In the African Homo lineage the same hmmmm sound has been divided into different meanings and marks the beginning of language as we know it today, around 200,000 years ago, which also marks the origin of the Homo sapiens. From this point onwards, there has been a divide in the meaning of communication into music and language. We still do not know how it precisely took place, but it was the dawn of music and language—the former being an expression of emotions and the latter the transmission of information. This shift, or split, of the humble hmmmm into a communicational system of emotion or information is due to the advanced cognition and increasing brain power of Homo sapiens and has benefited from a long evolutionary path. In light of this, the shift between music and language is not yet clear, and it would appear that with an appreciation of music being embedded in our genetic code, music had to come prior to language. This however remains speculation, and scholars up to the present day are still in disagreement about this development.

3

FROM MOLECULES
TO STREAMING SERVICES

As music plays such an embedded role in our genome, it should come as no surprise that throughout the existence of humanity we have longed for musical performances. Whether staging a recital in one's home (for the wealthy), or more simply in gatherings around fires, in the streets or in any good ol'e public house, music making and listening has been at the heart of social gatherings. But besides concerts and our urge, developed over the centuries, to be immersed in live music, humans have also increasingly wanted to own their music, ascribing to it the status of artefact. As we know, music, unlike other art forms, produces no lasting artefact. The music is out there, played, heard and disappears again, only leaving us with the memory and the emotion of what we have just experienced. This has changed with the rise of recordings and subsequently streaming. We no longer have to go and see a concert, engage in a musical performance during a pub visit, or call on our 'up-stairs' friends hosting a soirée, in order to enjoy our favourite song, opera or composition.

The rise of vinyl, the iPod, or any streaming service has allowed us to believe that music is important. But this is overcast by various money-making schemes which hide the actual importance of the arts and music. Different advances in technology and ways of recording have resulted in bringing music closer to ownership and away from memory. This does not necessarily have to be a bad thing, but with freedom and ownership comes great responsibility, a responsibility we too often turn away from. But let us assume that we all do take our responsibilities seriously, as we understand the way in which we live is a delicate balance between taking and giving and sharing with the people around us, near and far. So how did we get here, into this position of creating an artefact out of a heart artefact lacking an art form? Walk down any Western-inspired and influenced high street and you will notice people from all walks of life wearing earbuds or headphones, many of them with the iconic white Apple earbuds, which have been synonymous with the digital music revolution ever since the first adverts in 2000.

As early as 1877, music started to be transformed from a 'written' art, understood by few or solely played from memory, to a recorded representation in the form of Thomas Edison's phonograph. Music could now be recorded and played back. This has revolutionised music consumption as we know it today. Before Edison, there were multiple unsuccessful attempts to record music, but the year 1877 saw the first ever machine that was able to record and play back. The phonograph cylinder and playback stylus or needle could read the recording and play it back through the iconic horn. Edison continued to develop the idea and in 1889 the first wax cylinders were introduced so that the recorded sounds could be 'engraved' into the wax. In the 1890s, the cylinder was replaced by discs made of shellac, which was only supplanted by vinyl after World War II. The transition to vinyl came with a shift in the industry standard from 78 rounds per minute (rpm) to 33.3 rpm, allowing much larger amounts of music to be recorded on a single disc. Ten-inch 78 rpm could contain only three minutes of music, while 12-inch 33 rpm could hold as much as twenty minutes of music on each side. Changes beyond this point were mostly made to the hardware.

Even though radio technology began to be used commercially in 1900, music only appeared on the radio sometime between 1912 and 1917. After World War I and the suspension of amateur radio stations, music was rebroadcast again from around 1919. Lectures, the weather, classical concerts and other shows were broadcast live through the radio. Even though the advent of the radio brought a piece of the world into the home, the 'wireless' was expensive and it took some time before radios could be incorporated into every home. Before that people visited neighbours who could afford one, or gathered in public houses.

In 1958, the Radio Corporation of America revolutionised the future of home music consumption by introducing the RCA tape cartridge, which was a much larger version of the later popular compact cassette. The technology took some time to take off, but in 1960, the 8-track tape took the market by storm and the first really portable and owned music carrier was born, with 8-track players even in cars in the 1960s and '70s. The year 1979 saw the advent of the portable stereo tape player, also known as the Walkman. Music could now be listened to everywhere. Only a few years later, in 1983, cassettes outsold vinyl for the first time and shortly afterwards the first commercial compact disc (CD) appeared on the market. Even though digital recording had been around since the 1960s, CDs from the 1980s were standardised making them much easier for manufacturers to produce music. With the CD came the advent of portable CD players, CD changers, innovative laser technology and re-writable CDs (CD-RW), which superseded the recordable CD (CD-R) in the mid-1990s. CDs also made their way into the computer industry through CD read-only memory (CD-ROM) and into photo CDs, digital video discs (DVD), Blu-ray discs and, last but not least, the MiniDiscs (MD). All of this has happened over a relatively short space of time, within a meagre fifty-year period.

This revolution was born not only with technological advances, but also with marketing, sales and identity branding. In 1981, MTV, the first music television station, was launched to promote and share music, changing the face of music from an auditory to a mixed visual medium, where the music video received the same degree of status as the music itself. One could argue that this change had already been introduced by The Beatles and their performance on the Ed Sullivan Show in 1964, which marked the *saleability* of both music and its performance to a wider audience. But this discussion exceeds the scope and purpose of this short summary.

Karl-Heinz Brandenburg, who was an electrical engineering PhD at the Friedrich-Alexander University in Erlangen-Nürnberg (Germany), in 1982 was given a challenge to find a way to transmit music over a digital phone line. In order to do so, sound had to be broken down into three layers, each of which could be either discarded or saved depending on the importance of the sound. By taking advantage of a psychoacoustic phenomenon, auditory masking, Brandenburg and his associates were able to compress the file size of the recording. Auditory masking happens when the human ear is unable to hear certain sounds, and can therefore be discarded for the recording, shrinking the size of the file significantly. The Motion Picture Experts Group (MPEG), tasked with creating standards in audio recording, was created by the International Standards Organisation in 1988, which saw the advent of MPEG layers I, II and III, the last being of the highest quality. The work on these layers has naturally known multiple setbacks; however, MPEG-I Layer III was finalised in 1998 and has resulted in massive improvements in quality and the simplification of codes, as well as average and variable bitrate encoding. With the growth of the internet parallel to this development, with music-sharing platforms such as Napster, LimeWire and peer-to-peer file shares, desktop applications like Winamp, iTunes player and VLC increased in popularity. Different file extensions were created and associated with different bit rates and quality of operating systems. The extension .mp3 was decided upon in 1995, and is still used today. By 1996, the MP3 had moved from the desktop computer into your pocket in the format of MP3 players in all different sizes and shapes.

The year 2001 saw the birth of the iPod and with it the start of a new revolution. With the iPod a whole infrastructure was built around the music industry, where you could buy your favourite tunes or albums and transfer them directly (still via cable) to your device. Since 2001, the iPod has changed significantly and with the arrival of the Smart phone revolution, even the successful iPod has been thrown off its throne of best-selling and most-used music playing device.

It is quite difficult to award the title *first music service*; however, Pandora was launched in 2005 as one of the first on the market.

Five years before Pandora became a reality, the Music Genome Project was founded in an attempt to *capture the essence of music at the most fundamental level.* These characteristics included 'unique instruments', 'a lot of cymbals', 'hard rock roots' or anything else one could musically think of and were assigned by human analysis in order to identify the DNA of the music and consequently translated into an algorithm, which would search for music fitting this description in a song, album or whole music library. This approach has led to a kind of discovery engine, introducing millions of listeners to thousands of bands, songs and styles across the world. Algorithms, machine learning and artificial intelligence algorithms have informed the creation of Spotify, YouTube, Tidal and many more. Besides being able to quickly access a monumental amount of music, the biggest advantage of streaming services, such as Pandora, Spotify or even YouTube, is that they do not need terabytes of hard drive space to store information; however, and this is an often overlooked fact, they leave an immense CO_2 footprint and are one of the biggest contributors to global warming with all their data centres running 24/7.[10]

We have thus arrived at the crossroads of how music consumption has changed our experience and appreciation of music. One can argue that by recording music we have inflicted on ourselves the changeover in music from its actual necessity to our well-being, to a luxury product. As we can have it everywhere, whenever and with whomsoever we wish, it has become yet another form of consumerism, which takes away the importance of what music really means and evokes in human beings. I am not saying that this meaning exists in the music itself, but it is found in the experiences, memories and emotions it triggers and carries in relation to our own episodic and autobiographical memory. As mentioned above, we know very well which tunes to listen to or imagine when we wish to make ourselves more happy or sad. Nonetheless, it seems that we have reduced music down to just that, a means of manipulating our emotions. Something that will play in the background when *we* need it. Long gone are the days when music was so much more than a representation of little grooves on a round vinyl or 0011010101101 on a digital disc. We have turned music into yet another product we can choose to use or ignore, as we please. We can simply reduce it to its individual building blocks of melody or rhythm, major or minor, without any social, emotional or cognitive purpose whatsoever. The choice is yours; will you take the blue pill or the red pill—return to consumerism and believe all the fear, uncertainty and doubt (FUD) created by the current marketing propaganda and public relations about music and music making, or is it time to turn the page and reinvest in the arts, music, creativity and improvisation?

4
TO CREATE SOMETHING
OUT OF THIN AIR

The term improvisation has its origin in the Latin word *improvises*, which can be translated as 'unforseen' or 'unrehearsed'. *The Harvard Dictionary of Music* defines improvisation as a musical product, which is made without the aid of manuscript sketches, notation or memory. Such a definition suggests that improvisation creates something out of nothing. Elaborating on this, it would mean that we would be some sort of absolute creator in our own universe, with all the powers at our disposal to create and choose. But is this really how improvisation works? What it means to improvise? The example of an absolute creator is of course an over exaggeration, and we know very well that on the one hand it is more complicated than that and on the other much simpler.

Yet, in this book, I want to explore exactly this question: what is improvisation, how does it work, and why do we feel so uncomfortable when somebody asks us to improvise?

Improvisation seems to be one of the most researched, yet simultaneously most incomprehensible, phenomena in music. Very often, the terms 'freedom' and 'control' are used in conjunction with improvisation. According to musician and musicologist Aart van Bergen, the limitations as well as the freedom—for example, in jazz improvisation—stems from the musicians' sensitivity to "each other's interpretation of the framework and therefore the creation of something new" (van Bergen, 2007: 42). From a neuroscientific or cognitive point of view, however, it is much more difficult to define terms like 'freedom' or 'control' when it comes to improvisation and cognitive processes at large. Against this backdrop, the act of improvisation is reduced to a series of functions and becomes a *cognitive juggling exercise*, which allows for the *creatio ex nihilo*—the creation of something out of thin air. It is a very delicate balance, between knowing, doing and imagining, which on the one hand stems from our innate ability to be creative and interpret the world around us from the perspectives that we are used to and, on the other, draws from the more structured and scientific approaches that can explain a phenomenon such as improvisation. Why do we have the tendency to use cognition, the neurosciences or science in general to understand aesthetics, the arts, music and improvisation? Shouldn't we just leave the arts for what they are: an enrichment of our lives, a form of expression or an important pastime?

Maybe ...

However, leaving things for what they are only plays into the hands of individuals who claim that they certainly enjoy the arts, music and a free jazz improvisation that *others* create, but deny themselves a spot among the Greats. *Sure*, I hear you say, *Me, among the Greats of Coltrane, Bach, Górecki or Davis?!* But for one moment, just look at it from a different perspective: improvisation is an expression of emotions. It allows us to interact with our surroundings in varied ways and to some extent is aesthetically of a high value. Yet this does not mean that you cannot do it, that one cannot improvise. Bringing the neurosciences and cognitive sciences into this equation can help us paint the picture of how we, and yes you as well, can learn to improvise. It gives us the tools to not only analyse the way in which improvisation works, but also find the overlaps of our neural and cognitive working mechanism and apply them to the way we learn, create and, finally, improvise. They allow us to debunk the urban myth that we cannot improvise. Improvisation is a combination of multiple factors, an elegant dance between our culture, history and biology and their associated cognitive connections which we have made over our lifetime. From birth, until the day we leave this earth, we accumulate experiences—musical, personal, emotional—all of which make up the fabric that we call our consciousness or ourselves. We carry this heavy backpack and it helps us to define and understand the world around us and our perceptions of that world. We keep developing, growing, accumulating, interpreting and changing.

Improvisation is not about producing, or reproducing for that matter, an aesthetic product such as a musical piece. It is, as mentioned earlier, the ability to create something on the spur of the moment and apply it to the current situation. Looking at it in this way, improvisation is more of an organic perpetuum mobile, a sort of organism which spontaneously lays golden eggs from nothing—the *creatio ex nihilo*. For argument's sake, let us just adopt the stance of the *creatio ex nihilo*, the creation out of thin air, for a moment. How can we interpret improvisation and how should it be understood? We quickly fall into a never-ending philosophical spiral of why the chicken crossed the road. Each improvisation has to have an origin, something from where it came. It is very much comparable to the birth of our universe, the Big Bang: how could everything that we know and see in the whole universe be created out of nothing during the very early quantum fluctuations in the inflation field? But I am digressing. Researcher Bruce Benson bases his understanding of improvisation on pre-learned parameters and experiences within a context. These parameters are memorised—consciously or subconsciously—and can then be used in any given moment. What a wonderful segue into the world of transistors, hard drives, cables, electrical impulses and networks, which we have at our disposal: our brains.

5
RESEARCHING
IMPROVISATION

Improvisation has been researched in many ways throughout the years. Nonetheless, the discussion around combining systematic, historical and cognitive musicology has been one of the key debates in music-related research. Looking at improvisation in a musical context, and how we can gain a greater understanding of the ways in which we actually improvise and why we do so, multiple methodological problems arise, as we have to amalgamate culture, biology, philosophy and aesthetics under one methodological banner. This, however, is a challenge that science has already faced in the twenty-first century. We must look beyond our own discipline to understand how things are connected and how they relate to each human individually, but also to humanity and the world at large. Science is no longer something happening in a lab behind closed doors, with highbrow discussions in ivory towers; it is the link allowing the actual implementation of academic problems into society, sharing experiences, knowledge and views. To this end, let me share the *Mind the Music* playlist[11] with you, which will accompany us throughout this book.

In order to paint the picture of improvisation and, to a certain extent, convince you that you too are able to improvise, we will discuss different models from different disciplines, propose extensions to these, and engage in the discourse of improvisation together. Consequently, improvisation is a shared responsibility of aesthetics.

Looking at improvisation, we can see it from different perspectives. We have already briefly mentioned the cognitive and the aesthetic. However, from an anthropological viewpoint, we would have to examine improvisation in its cultural context: the cultural background and fabric into which it is interwoven. 'Traditional' neuroscience usually does not look at the cultural background, as it could muddy the interpretation of results. This, however, and coming from a neuroscientist, is an incomplete way to look at a phenomenon such as improvisation. We cannot simply look at brain function and cognition and expect this to solve the how, why and what of improvisation. We have to look at its embedment into the socio-cultural background of each individual, as well as the overall social and cultural context. Additionally, we must consider the cultural and social background of each surrounding within which we learn to improvise. Different cultures have different ways of teaching and especially of teaching how to improvise. Thus, speaking of improvisation and, to a certain extent, of freedom in improvisation, we will look at the social and cultural world we inhabit (ontology) and how we acquire knowledge, what that knowledge encompasses, and how we know what we know about improvisation (epistemology). Approaching the issue in this way will allow us to, hopefully, take away the fear some of us carry when it comes to the actual act.

6
ART-BASED OR CLINICAL RESEARCH: TWO SIDES OF THE SAME COIN?

Throughout this book, we will look at improvisation from different perspectives, two of which are the artistic and the clinical.

To reinvent and redefine research within the domain of music and improvisation, we have to consider other domains in order to understand improvisation as a whole. Only when we see the similarities across domains, whether it is the arts, medicine, the humanities or philosophy, can we embrace the differences and add them to the way we understand music and improvisation at large. This can be achieved by sharing methods and methodologies and exchanging the blueprints of research unique to each discipline.

Clinical research may share questions with art-based research, but both come from very diverse professional contexts. Normality/abnormality, diagnosis, frequency, risk, prognosis and treatment are very different whether we ask a medical doctor, an artist or a philosopher.

Clinical or lab-based research investigates abnormalities, risks or prognoses using interventions and experiments. Art-based research may view such problems in a more community-based context or see how they fit into cultural or societal beliefs. As such, art-based research identifies the *existential need* for art and the amount of it needed for it to be effective, assessing risks for artists, the listener and the surroundings, and possibly even making a prognosis or advocating for change in a turbulent society. Considering this, do clinical research and art-based research even ask the same questions? Not only do both types of research co-exist, but they are also co-dependent, as we have to understand a certain problem from different angles in order to grasp it fully.

As professionals, both artists and clinicians invest a lot of time in the observation of art, their clients/patients and the trends and developments within their respective fields. Based on these observations, we make certain assumptions and try to prove or disprove them within the context known to us. As an example, in 1796, Franz Josef Gall[12] coined the term and discipline of phrenology. Although now regarded as an obsolete amalgamation of primitive neuroanatomy with moral philosophy, phrenology was widely used amongst nineteenth-century psychologists and psychiatrists, even well into the twentieth century. In short, phrenology focused on personality and character traits by measuring the size, weight and shape of the human skull. Each dent or bulge in a skull was associated with a specific personality type which, in turn, had caused it. Even though it is a fascinating and sometimes amusing subject, phrenology is an elegant example of association and assumption not working out.

We need evaluation and observation to make sure we are measuring the exact thing that we want to know. Through the use of phrenology, Gall did not measure cognition or personality—it was simply a glorified way to look at how big somebody's head was.

This example is important when it comes to researching music and improvisation. We can look at the instruments, the length of the tune, and the highs and lows; but will this tell us everything about improvisation? We have to also explore the way in which we understand it within the context of society, technology, neuroscience and other disciplines related to the subject of improvisation and music, rather than a single discipline.

It goes without saying that by combining various fields in the exploration of a subject, we can see it in all its facets. We can therefore merge views from the arts and the medical profession, creating a beautiful symbiosis. The arts—in this case, primarily the visual arts—in medical education can significantly support professionals to train their 'clinical eye'. Scientists Shapiro, Rucker and Beck investigated whether medical students develop better clinical observational abilities when receiving lessons in which they evaluated and talked about works of art. A group of thirty-eight third-year students was divided into a medical group, working with clinical photographs and paper cases, and a group working with paintings and dance. Whereas students in the clinical group could transfer their skills directly to the medical field (a phenomenon called 'near transfer'), students in the art-based group developed observational skills *beyond* the required 'medical eye', such as emotion recognition, cultivation of empathy, identification of story and narrative, and awareness of multiple perspectives. These skills may not be a required aspect of a 'traditional' medical education; however, they allow for a different view of the same problem, stimulating creativity and strengthening the ability to improvise, falling into the category of 'far transfer' learning, where learning skills in one domain influence skills in an unrelated domain. This process of unrelated skill learning shows that "the interventions studied [both clinical as well as the arts] were naturally complementary and, taken together, can bring greater texture to the process of teaching clinical medicine by helping us see a more complete 'picture' of the patient" (Shapiro, Rucker & Beck, 2006:263). Using the arts to train medical professionals in their observational skills is one example of how the arts can be utilised beyond intervention; however, this link is often not easily made.

7
MUSIC AND THE BRAIN

Before we take a more in-depth look at how the brain processes music, and how these processes relate to improvisation, let us place the *music* centre stage and inspect it under a magnifying glass. Music touches us (quite literally). It triggers emotions and evokes memories, it can change our mood, makes us cry, and is used in various healthcare settings from neonatal intensive care units to dementia. Music and the application of music is so extensive that we will have to limit ourselves here when it comes to improvisation.

I suggest we let the music speak for itself and invite you to listen to the song 'What We Have' by contemporary American musician Sean Jones. What do you hear? Piano, trumpet, double-bass, saxophone and drums. Together they form a piece of music, which, even though we might not have heard this piece before, evokes an emotion. If we do know it, maybe a memory is triggered? Together they form what is called an association, whether from memory (we have heard the tune before and are re-experiencing certain moments associated with it: associated memory) or in the case of never having heard it before, we are making new associations, linking them to the current moment. We could of course take a brain scan to determine what and why you have or make a certain association, or we could look at it from a musicologist point of view: what musical structure is imposed, what is the role of the instruments and their associated tone colours and voices, and in which historical context can we place them? However, these would only focus on a small part of how you experience this piece of music.

8
SOCIO-CULTURAL CONTEXT

It clearly is more than just the brain, or just history or musicology. To understand music and improvisation, we also have to understand the background of the musicians, where they come from, and what traditions they have learnt and used to play the music. This of course is next to impossible, as each individual carries their own memories, perceptions and thoughts, all informed by, but not exclusive to, upbringing, social background and personality. Nevertheless, we must be aware of the culture or social fabric of the music and the musicians we are listening to. Looking at a piece of art or listening to music with our own eyes and ears will obviously create a bias from our own pool of knowledge. Yet we should try to step into another's shoes, try to see the world with their eyes, and listen to music with their ears and their understanding. It is about realising that in order to engage with any art form, we need to have a basic understanding of the culture from which it originated, as we are being invited to experience their world. Only when we are aware of the different facets that music entails, can we understand its importance in our lives, to society, to well-being, or to any other entity that music encompasses.

At this stage, I must admit that a complete understanding of music will remain an illusion, as it is next to impossible to comprehend the totality of something as complex as music. However, we will try our utmost to shed light on this complex multi-sensory stimulus: a stimulus which triggers memory, emotion and cognition. To add another level of complexity to an already complex phenomenon, and move beyond the bodily sensations that music triggers, let us look at the term 'music' itself and the multiple ways in which it can be used. For example, someone in an orchestra is asking for the *music*, which would imply the score or instrumental part written down on a piece of paper; or people are proud of their *music* collection, which refers to the actual quantity of their CDs, LPs or MP3s. *Music* can also be understood as an agent of social interaction and/or identification with a certain group. Ultimately, in the context of *music*, we can see improvisation as a dialogue with other musicians, the audience or the composer's notation, should the musicians choose to deviate from it. All of these are different ways in which the term *music* is used and what it means, depending on the context, with an external representation like physical numbers, clothing or social environment. Music, therefore, is a complex whole, with an auditory core and several individually self-sustaining factors being pulled in by its force of gravity. Having presented this far from complete list of some meanings of the term *music*, shouldn't we abandon the socio-cultural or historical input altogether, and just focus on brain and cognition for the sake of simplicity? The idea here is not to reduce music and its associations to a simplified version to fit the bill. It is about raising the awareness of its cultural and historical context in neuroscience and psychology. Understanding music and improvisation from a cultural point of view, the way it is acquired, learned and passed on, will in turn help us to untangle the complex processes of the brain, and even provide us with examples easier to relate to, than abstract concepts such as intelligence, mind and thought.

9
MUSIC AS A
MULTISENSORY STIMULUS

Music is a multisensory stimulus: an impulse which activates multiple senses and thus brain functions in a wide array of areas and connections. It is therefore impossible to reduce music to a single brain area or a single connection in the brain. The incoming musical signal triggers multiple areas in order to create the experience of listening to music. Multisensory means that the central nervous system can trigger different senses, such as sight, smell, hearing, taste and balance, and integrate them into one input–output signal. This means that all of the senses have to be activated in order to understand the incoming input, before it can be distributed across the brain's network, starting a selection process as to which senses have to remain active, which can be disregarded after a first initiation, and how to proceed towards an understanding of the input and what to do with it (output). Multisensory integration is one of the key aspects of an organism to adapt itself to its environment and perceive the world as a whole, rather than in its individual components. Against this backdrop, it is not quite certain whether this is something unique to humans, as research has shown that dogs remember by storing individual components of their environment, i.e., only smell, only visual, only auditory. It is not clear whether they reintegrate this information into their perception of the world. As humans we have the ability to shift between such states, remembering just a smell, or just a sound; however, this is quickly taken over by the multisensory integration network, which is looking for the correct representation of the remembered stimulus in order to create as comprehensive a picture of it as possible. To illustrate this, let us look at an everyday example. Imagine you are walking into a traditional bakery. The first thing that hits you, as soon as you open the door, will be the smell of freshly baked bread, rolls and other tasty things. You are taking a deep breath in through your nose to savour this lovely aroma. In the background you see the staff working the dough, you feel the warmth of the oven as it radiates into the room. While reading this short passage, you have most likely been transported back to that bakery, remembering the smell of fresh bread and maybe even the taste. It may even have triggered an emotion or particular feeling. Now imagine you are touching the bread. The surface is still warm, it has just been resting for a few minutes after it has been taken out of the oven. You pick it up, breaking it in half, making a fresh cracking noise, releasing the moist warmth of the inside which fills your nostrils. You close your eyes, allowing the warmth in your hands, the smell, and the sound of the bread to consume you, and suddenly you see yourself sitting at the table of your grandmother, where you are handed a buttered slice of freshly made bread and you indulge in the taste and the warm feeling associated with that memory.

"Excuse me, would you mind paying please, there are other customers waiting."

This scenario exemplifies multisensory integration—multiple stimuli being processed simultaneously, triggering emotions, memories and behaviour. Music and, even more so, improvisation rest exactly on this concept of multisensory integration.

In 1965, Milton Babbitt proposed a view of psychological music representations derived from the acoustic or physical, the auditory or perceived, and the graphemic or notated domain. Babbitt himself was an American composer, music theorist and teacher, and he spent his life searching for the meeting point between the arts, technology and the mind. With his psychological representations of music, Babbitt has opened a Pandora's box in trying to understand the different facets of music, as none of the described domains encompass music in all its beauty. In the years since, our comprehension of music as a cognitive representation has fundamentally changed and has been defined as music and musicality, emphasising a general (human) interest in music.

10

MUSIC AS WAVES
AND FREQUENCIES

A complex stimulus, such as music, consists of different layers. In a physical sense it is made up of waves, which are the key to understanding frequencies. Tracing this representation of music back to its origins, we will arrive at the beginning of time, at the beginning of the cosmos itself. It was around 13.8 billion years ago when wavelengths, particles and subsequent atoms were first formed, all of which contribute to a physical representation of sound. In the end, sound, and therefore music, is nothing more or less than waves travelling through air, with different frequencies and amplitudes which touch our ear drums. It is the organisation of sound, of waves and frequencies, which allows the music to be understood by our brains, as well as explaining our physiological reactions to it. The organisation of frequencies, regardless of tonality or atonality, are therefore perceived and encompass every sonic wave, i.e., rhythm, pitch, melody, timbre and harmony. To this end, each wavelength is related to a specific frequency. At a constant speed of sound, frequency (the number of wave crests per second) is exactly inversely proportional to wavelength. One does not lead the other, meaning that frequency and wavelength cannot be seen as waves forming frequencies and frequencies as the base of waves. Let us illustrate this with a musical example. If we take the A above the middle C on the piano, and we assume that the piano is tuned to the currently accepted *kamerton* or reference pitch, we will measure a frequency of 440 Hz. Based on this 440 Hz, the piano can be tuned, which will give the illusion of the piano being in tune, or tonal. Should you suffer or be blessed with perfect pitch, which is the ability to name each note at any given moment on any given instrument or object, you will struggle with listening to a piano, as the higher notes are not perfectly in tune with the reference pitch regardless of the frequency. This derives from the way a piano is built, the resonance of each tone, and the multiple strings representing middle and higher tones when hit by the hammer. Hence, we have the *illusion* of tonality.

The frequency of 440 Hz has not always been referred to as the reference pitch and different frequencies have been used. Until the nineteenth century there was no consensus as to what the reference pitch should be at all, which often resulted in the most interesting combinations of pitches. The tuning of instruments on the same continent, in the same country, or even in the same city could vary hugely. Two different church organ pipes in the same city could have been tuned in a completely different way, up to five half tone steps apart. The reason for this was not only the lack of consensus about the reference pitch, but also the way church organ pipes were tuned. To tune a pipe, one has to gently hammer the bottom and top ends of the pipe to either increase or decrease the cone shape, which results in either a higher or lower pitch, respectively. Through this rather hands-on tuning process, the bottom and top parts of the pipes became more and more damaged, so much so that in order to be able to play and tune the organ without replacing the whole pipe, the clerk had to cut or repair the frayed edges, resulting in a change in pitch. This can sometimes still be seen on old church organ pipes; the next time you wander into a cathedral and the organist is playing, simply ask them about this phenomenon.

Early in the eighteenth century, one could also determine pitch with the tuning fork invented in 1711. From this date, it was finally possible to determine the differences between pitches. Of course, tuning forks were tuned differently, resulting in the tuning fork associated with Händel's music to be tuned in the frequency of A = 422.5 Hz. A later tuning fork model manufactured in 1780 was tuned to A = 409 Hz, which is about a quarter tone lower. Towards the end of the eighteenth century, the tuning fork varied between A = 400 Hz to A = 450 Hz. These precise descriptions are of course based on modern measurements, so one can only imagine the cacophony of tuning fork pitches that were used in those days depending on the hearing, age and skill of the manufacturer. We do not know whether the different frequencies were common knowledge to musicians in those days, although we do know that Marine Mersenne created a rough estimation of different sound frequencies in the seventeenth century. Scientific measurements were not performed until the nineteenth century, when German physicist Johan Scheibler accurately assessed and evaluated those frequencies. Nowadays, we measure frequencies in Hertz. The term Hertz has not always been used in the description of frequencies. The first measure was introduced as *cycles per second* or CPS, and was only replaced in the twentieth century by the unit Hertz (1 Hz is equal to 1 CPS), named so after the German physicist Rudolf Hertz.

The gradual increase in pitch, and thus in frequency, originates in the growing popularity of instrumental music during the Renaissance and Baroque periods. Instrumentalists wanted to perfect their personal sound as well as reaching a more *brilliant* sound. This is actually possible on string instruments by increasing the tension on the strings and thus increasing the pitch very slightly so as to stay in the tonal range but give the instrument's sound just that tiny edge of *brilliance*. Understandably, this practice has not found favour with the vocalists, who plead for a standardisation of reference pitch in order to be able to play and sing together. This dispute has resulted in multiple angry discussions and even riots across France during the Renaissance and Baroque periods. To avoid further quarrels, the French government was forced to decide on one standardised frequency, which was agreed at C = 435 Hz. Their (forced) initiative was the first on record and has become known as the *diapason normal* or *French reference pitch*.

During the nineteenth and twentieth centuries, there were multiple attempts to change the pitch again: 256 Hz has become known as the *philosophical* or *scientific reference pitch*. However, an alternative way of tuning has never really found a common ground, even though Giuseppe Verdi always composed his music 'lower' than the French reference pitch.

Today most orchestras use the agreed standard reference pitch of 440 Hz; however, there are also the odd ones out, who believe that an alternative pitch contributes to their particular sound, like the New York Philharmonic, the Boston Symphony Orchestra or the Dutch Royal Concertgebouw Orchestra, who all tune in A = 442 Hz. German orchestras often tune in 443 Hz, the Lithuanian Chamber Orchestra in Wilnus uses 444 Hz and the English Baroque Soloists a tuning of A = 430 Hz. Which frequency is the best lies in the ear of the listener.[13]

One thing however is certain; the mythical frequency of 432 Hz, which often is referred to as the frequency of the universe, is more science fiction than science. Theories encompassing this universal frequency have not yet found empirical proof, and given that over the centuries different tunings have been used, the chances that people over time have perceived the world differently, necessitating a variety of frequencies, argues against a sole universal frequency.

11
MUSIC AS ORGANISED SOUND

We have seen that music consists of waves and that these waves correspond with frequencies, which in turn create a tone or pitch. Following this train of thought down the rabbit hole, we can say that music is nothing more or less than a chain of individual frequencies, like pearls on a necklace, bound together to form one entity. We can therefore say that the result we call music is a conscious organisation and structuring of frequencies or sounds. Each *structuring*, however, knows sub-structures. For this reason, a complex stimulus like music consists of ever deeper layers. Each tone consists of micro tones, and each micro tone is in turn divided into cents. Each micro tone resonates with a certain frequency and contributes to the sounding of the tone or pitch, which we perceive as either A or C, or any other pitch. It is comparable to the piano string example above, where each tone on the middle and higher register consists of two or three strings in order to make the sound, each of the strings being tuned slightly differently to create the desired note. While this example upscales our understanding of pitch, microtonality looks at it from the other end of the spectrum. Each pitch or tone consists of microtones, in the same way that each atom consists of ever smaller particles, all the way down to the Higgs boson or even quark. Like an atom, musical tones or pitches know ever smaller units. Research into the effects of microtones or even smaller particles, which imprint the pitch on perception, is still in its infancy. It is likely that microtones, which we really only perceive subconsciously or passively as our hearing is not sensitive enough to detect them individually, can have a profound effect on the way we hear something. Think of the earlier discussion on the different reference pitches. Changing the reference pitch from 440 Hz to 442 Hz, or 443.5 Hz, will not make a huge difference in listening, unless we put two orchestras next to each other and let them play the exact same piece simultaneously. Only then we might be able to hear that the two are out of tune with each other. And yet, there is something different in the way we listen to either a performance by the New York Philharmonics or the London Sinfonietta, and it is not always due to the musicians, the conductor, or the interpretation of the piece played.

Besides the anatomy of the tone, the already mentioned cultural and social building blocks of music add to the complexity of perception. Music as organised sound is not just its individual hearable components, but how we understand as well as interpret those (micro)tones in a wider context. Music is a continuously changing construct, whether cultural or sonic, comprising meaning, emotion and memory, but also pitch, rhythm and harmony. It is like watching a play, where different actors play their role to tell the story.

But just imagine for a moment that you do not speak the language, understand the grammar or even the context of what you are seeing. Imagine that you have been invited to a tiny village in the south of rural China, where the local population is celebrating the Chinese New Year with a vast theatrical performance. The performance, however, knows its own symbols, meanings and interpretations, which can only be understood by the local population. You are trying to follow the plot, your Mandarin is not up to speed and your friend who speaks it fluently also struggles to understand the words. You keep asking yourself, neither understanding the words nor the context, what the symbols and movements mean. You are faced with two choices now, either sit back and let yourself be enchanted, or try to interpret the events from your Western perspective of theatre performances, coupled with what you have read about China and Chinese culture. You ask your friend to help you, but she can give you only a very broad context, imposing her own assumptions onto the performance, as she is not local to this village but resides in the North. Your expectations, both what will come next in the plot and what it could mean, will either be met or not met, and based on this experience you will discuss the performance with your friend on your way back home: what have we just witnessed?

We do not, however, have to catch a plane to China to experience such an event. A similar scenario could take place in the Globe Theatre in London. While standing in the rain watching Shakespeare's *Macbeth*, even though we do not necessarily struggle with the language, as the performance is in English, and we might have some basic knowledge of the plot, we will not understand all the jokes and meanings of the words. The language used during a medieval performance sounds English, and is English, but is often further from the English we know than we may imagine, as the meanings of words, expressions and idioms have evolved from what they once were. In this Shakespeare example, we might feel more like our Chinese friend, who tried to explain and understand the southern Chinese theatre performance from a northern perspective.

Our assumptions are more likely to be met and our anticipation of what will come next be satisfied, but we are still not quite convinced whether or not we have understood the whole plot correctly.

When it comes to improvisation, we are facing a similar dilemma: if we do not know which building blocks make up music, or how these elements come together in a sonic, cultural or social framework, we will not understand what comprises the glue that keeps them together, or how to recognise improvisation as a *creatio ex nihilo*.

12
IMPROVISATION: TRADITION VERSUS INNOVATION

What is improvisation and what are the underlying elements which allow a performer to create a new 'masterpiece' by midnight, every night? It is influenced by culture and society, however, it also necessitates the mastery of the voice or instrument and knowledge of music theory.

All musical cultures know that improvisation is an important part. Whether it is the early Gregorian chants, Bach's Baroque music or Spanish Flamenco, all use a form of improvisation. To illustrate this, let us focus on two musical cultures, which rely on improvisation from the very beginning: the Hindustani music culture and the more or less 'traditional' conservatory jazz curriculum culture. In both, one needs to master the instrument or voice, and understand the music.

Farhan Khan, son of renowned sitar player Ustad Rais Khan, received his education on the sitar in a 'traditional' Hindustani sense—copying his father until he could develop his own musical voice. Although Hindustani music appears to be more experimental, tolerant of change, and with a broad interest in developing its music culture, compared to other Indian music traditions, improvisation is a central part of all Indian music. Hindustani music, however, is known to be more adventurous, moving away from traditional texts and representations. According to Kahn and ethno-musicologist Derek Bailey, Hindustani music keeps reinventing itself, being always on the lookout for innovation, transformation and change. Against this backdrop, Bailey acknowledges that moving away from 'tradition' does not mean moving away from heritage, which is part of the way music is understood and learnt. Bailey goes as far as saying that the performance of music, as well as acquiring ultimate proficiency on the instrument and a thorough grasp of theoretical knowledge, are indistinguishable from a book of religious instruction and has therefore a great effect on the spiritual experience of the musician. A spiritual experience cannot be learned, of course, but is the result of devotion to scripture, belief and love. However, when looking at the way music is taught in the Hindustani tradition, one quickly sees that devotion, belief and love go hand in hand with the artistic as well as with the divine. The student has to sit in front of the teacher (Kahn in front of his father) and copy everything that the teacher is playing, without questioning it. The pupil will not know whether what he does is correct or not, and thus has to develop a sense of what is right. While copying the master, the pupil learns various things: how to perform in a given context proposed by the master; how not to deviate from a set of rules and framework in order to understand and, even more so, feel the given musical moment; and last but certainly not least the musical voice of the master. This musical voice has been passed down from master to pupil for generations and has become inseparable from the music and the master's musical voice. Each master will undoubtedly influence that 'ancient musical tone', giving it a slight alteration, but past voices will remain in it, recognisable to the trained ear. This musical heritage, the different voices of past masters, will eventually become part of the student's musical vocabulary and influence and shape their own sound. It goes without saying that teachers or masters have a huge responsibility to understand and correctly convey their knowledge without half measures and shortcuts. Kahn, and every other student in the Hindustani tradition therefore, has to understand the way of the teacher and apply the framework of *sruti, svara, tala, laya, raga, alapa* and *gat*[14] into their vocabulary and, in turn, into their own musical voice.

13
IN SEARCH OF
YOUR OWN VOICE

Searching for your musical voice is similar to finding your own voice when speaking. We tend not to think about the way we use our voice, how we have acquired the sound of it, how our vocal cords have adapted and learned to open and close in order to create the unique voice we have. It may not come as a surprise that genetic factors mostly determine the sound of our voice as they influence the anatomy and size, length and shape of our larynx, body, mouth and tongue. This is the same for a musical instrument; the size, shape and material will determine the sound. However, as with instruments, so also with your voice, we cannot ignore the effect that the environment has on both shaping the sound of the voice and its early development. The way our parents have spoken to us and encouraged us to speak, as well as our surroundings, leave a profound mark on our voices. How this happens precisely is not fully understood, as it is a complex and delicate balance between multiple factors which contribute to our sonic identity

Nonetheless, we have acquired our sound when it comes to our voice. A similar phenomenon happens when musicians talk about their musical voice. As we have seen in the example of Farhan Kahn, and the way he was taught to play the sitar, he was copying the voices of all the masters who taught his father and made them part of his own voice and hence vocabulary. While engaging with different sounds and voices, every musician will gradually discover their own way of playing anatomically—the way we stand, sit or use our hands, and in turn the effect of this on our musical voice. Additionally, musical expressions like the use of vibrato, tremolo, warmth or touch will add to the way a musician sounds, regardless of voice or instrument. Adding to these different musical experiences, like playing together with different musicians, will influence the way we play and shape our sound even further.

Often forgotten are surgical and dental interventions, which can change your embouchure—the way a player applies their mouth to the mouthpiece of a wind or brass instrument. The mouth has learned to apply pressure in a certain way, and together with the teeth behind the lips has saved this movement and tension to muscle memory, which can be applied, when necessary, without great thought; this is something we call cognitive economy, but we will return to this later. Now imagine you undergo a jaw correction, or the dentist decides to take out your wisdom teeth or change the filling in a crown on your front teeth. All of these, somewhat minor interventions, change the way you use your mouth and lips and in turn violate the anticipation of your muscle memory; hence, they will require you to retrain your embouchure, which will have an effect on your initial sound and way of playing. The same could be said about accidents—think of Tony Iommi, famous guitarist of Black Sabbath. Tony lost his fingertips in a work accident, which, one could say, could make it impossible for him to play the guitar. However, listening to the song 'War Pigs' leaves us in no doubt that his accident did not impair Mr Iommi's ability to play in the slightest.

Every way of interacting with your instrument, combined with the abilities you have and the past voices you have internalised, will all contribute to your recognisable and embossed sonic fingerprint.

14

TEACHING TO LEARN
AND LEARNING TO TEACH

A similar way of teaching and learning is utilised in the 'traditional' conservatory jazz curriculum tradition. The student has to transcribe as many solos as possible of all the great jazz masters, so they know what is allowed to be played and what sounds good. These boundaries must be adhered to before moving away from them. I have caught myself quoting my double bass teacher, Dr Riaan Vosloo, from my time at Dartington College of the Arts, who repeatedly told me: you can break all the rules, but first learn them, otherwise they will simply not call you for the next gig. And good student that I was, I went on to break all the rules.

The conservatorium tradition demands that the novice memorise gradations of 'important' solos.

Thus, the eager student looks for all the solos ever played by their favourite bass player, Charles Mingus. Mingus's style and choice of notes will become part of the student's vocabulary. However, less obvious in the western jazz tradition is that all Mingus's predecessors, and the way in which Mingus has learned to play, will, to an extent, become part of the student's musical fingerprint. The more the student practises different transcriptions, the more these will slowly be incorporated into the memory of the novice, becoming part of their vocabulary and ultimately their musical voice.

It is believed that for the proper development of a musical voice it is paramount to know these parameters, to know what and how others have played and performed, and to memorise them in order to be successful in learning how to play and eventually improvise. Even though we need to know the boundaries and limitations of the musical discourse, we also have to allow for a certain amount of artistic freedom—to explore, to experiment and to look for exactly these limitations in order to go beyond them. In the end, we do not work music, we play.

Through this method of teaching, the information presented to and attained by the student is 'saved' to their memory, ready to be retrieved when needed. Here again cognitive economy peaks around the corner, applying information, when necessary, without great thought. This way of learning, of memorising, however, is a valid method of learning in a music academy, but also weakens the argument of those who think that improvisation is the creation of something out of thin air and strengthens the hypothesis that there is no truly free improvisation, only improvisation which is based on pre-learned musical fragments. It appears as if there is no alternative to learn how to improvise without having to 'copy somebody else's ideas' and therefore the convention and framework within which they operate. The good news is that this way of looking at it allows everybody to simply pick up an instrument, practise, copy everything they can possibly learn, and then improvise. This is something a machine-learning algorithm or an artificial intelligence prompt would do. The bad news, or maybe even better news, is that it is much more complicated than simply copying and pasting. One of the reasons why a computer—even with the impressive workings of the latest GUID Partition Table or ChatGPT 3—cannot improvise, in the same way humans improvise, is that the computer simply loses track after two sentences, spitting out gibberish. If it is trained to read a book, it can only remember parts of it and can reproduce only one chapter; having a lively conversation about the book will simply cause it to crumble. We expect our friends to remember what we talked about yesterday in the pub; a chatbot does not possess such a memory and, hence, is not able to link two conversations.

The recently launched ChatGPT 4 has made an impressive jump from its predecessor, merging text, video, audio, pictures and other information in its database and actually writes, composes and even paints beyond what ChatGPT3 could do. Is it creative? Can it improvise? No, as it is still based on existing knowledge biases and does not come up with novel ideas, at least not yet. The speed with which these algorithms are changing is impressive, and by the time this book is published there might be an improvisation algorithm outshining us all. So far, we have not reached Ray Kurzweil's Singularity[15] but by the time you are reading this, we just might have.

Improvisation is exactly this: a conversation in time and space, particular to a specific context, based on what we know, yet moving beyond its own limitations.

As human beings we are constantly in search of these limitations. We are looking for the boundaries of our knowledge, our ideas and our beliefs. We share this through words with others, reflecting together and sometimes alone, on what we think and want to convey. In some instances, it is a life-long search to discover what we want to say, how we want to see the world, and how the world perceives us in turn. All these changes, doubts and wishes are based on both what we learn and know and how we apply this knowledge—how we improvise to create something new. Improvisation seems to be imbedded into our genetic fabric as we do it without even being aware of it. We do it every day, in conversation. The way we use language, choose our words, and share them with others, is in itself an act of improvisation. We do this on the spot, when necessary, without thinking about it.

Let us return to the bakery scenario. You walk into the bakery, the smell hits you and you experience all the emotions conjured up by the aroma of freshly baked bread. However, there is one big difference from previously: the bakery has run out of the tasty white loaf you wanted and so you are forced to change your routine. You start to improvise, inquiring about other breads, whether they are as tasty as the one you always buy. We have to think on our feet, just like the Scouse waitress in Alexei Sayles's sketch, from the *Imaginary Sandwich Bar* series, who says: "we ran out of pitta, you want Hovis?" (2017).[16]

Over the course of our lives, we have gathered words, phrases and idioms into our vocabulary and can freely use them without having to think a lot about which word comes next. We have learned from copying our parents, their friends, uncles and aunts and later our peers, friends, colleagues, books we have read, movies we have seen and music we have heard. Whether we buy bread, or play in a big band, we are reacting to the world around us, with words or with notes. The act and, as we shall see, our brain connections, as well as our cognitive processes, are the same with some minor differences depending on the improvisational context.

15
FRAMED FREEDOM

In *Thinking in Jazz: The Infinite Art of Improvisation* (1994), Paul Berliner has written one of the most thorough defences of jazz and improvisation in the science of music. Berliner explores the tradition of musical creativity and improvisation from as many angles as possible, in and beyond the musical context. Investigating the problem from a cultural and social viewpoint, he asks the question how does improvisation impact us and society by challenging the views of musicians, who practise the act of improvisation every day. While this is a valuable point of departure, it begs another question: how are we, as non-professional musicians, able to improvise? Against this backdrop, Berliner strongly advocates the idea that improvisation is based on pre-learned concepts and parameters, which are applied in a given context and, thus, improvisation can never be an expression of ultimate freedom but a choice of pitches, rhythms and harmonies in a given tradition. This implies that simply learning every possible tune, solo or phrase will allow you to improvise, as you have an in-built comprehensive musical library. Jazz saxophone player Joshua Redman has put it another way: there are so many different solos and tunes out there that it is nearly impossible to choose the wrong notes or tunes to play in any given context.[17] According to him, we have to pick the ones we enjoy, the ones that touch us, and learn them by heart. Once we know them, write them down. Writing it down is as important as what you are writing down. Looking at improvisation as a combination of possibilities, rather than as an expression of freedom, seems to open up the discussion about it even more and, in turn, allows for different points of view about how we improvise. Having said that, jazz trumpet player Wynton Marsalis turns this around again and reminds us that jazz is not just "well, man, this is what I feel like playing; it is a very structured thing that comes down from a tradition and requires a lot of thought and study"[18] (Marsalis, 2010: 134–35). We could say that this very much reflects the more 'traditional' music academy view of jazz. But it is not so much about whether we learn music at an institution and are provided with the views of others because it fits a particular curriculum. It is more about understanding the language enough to say what we want to say, rather than what we intend to say. It also includes a tradition of listening to each other, to the people who have devoted their lives to something that exceeds our comprehension. This does not mean that we cannot learn to use this language—just look at the way you write and speak the more you read—; on the contrary, we are able to add new voices to our own voice and grow in the process. Musicians like Louis Armstrong and B.B. King learnt to play with and from others, and not necessarily from initially reading music. They did not write and transcribe their solos on paper, but played them, practised them, experimented with different voices in order to find their own context, their own voice and sound. Even when we analyse improvisation from a more music scientific or musicological perspective, the plot thickens further. Musicologist Ingrid Monson has looked at the different roles musicians have in a band and how they relate to improvisation and the part they play in the band (*Saying Something: Jazz Improvisation and Interaction*, 1997). She divides these into the rhythm section (piano, drums and bass) and the front line or melody line (brass, wind and vocals). Everybody in the band has their role to play whether it is accompanying, leading or accentuating. These three roles can of course be interchanged, and each instrument or section can be put in the spotlight. However, we have to know when, how and where this can happen in the Big Band environment, otherwise everybody would start and stop at random, which would create a room full of people all talking at the same time, rather than a musical conversation. Monson further stresses that only when one knows the boundaries, can one move beyond them and create something outside the rhythmic, harmonic, dynamic and melodic relationship within the given context—the illusion of freedom within a set framework.

16
IMPROVISATION AS DIALOGUE

Music and language researcher Bruce Benson has brought the idea of breaking beyond the boundaries of a given context even further in his book, *The Improvisation of Musical Dialogue: A Phenomenology of Music* (2009). Benson states that improvisation and therefore expressions within a given context can be divided into a variety of types and degrees of improvisation. Despite the fact that his list is not complete, he presents different degrees of improvisation. The first stage of these variations happens at the basic level of minimalistic changes in tempo, attack, dynamics and, to some extent, instrumentation, i.e., which instruments are chosen and how they are played, and the expectation of the sound they produce—the beginning of the sound of the musical voice. Adding to this is the choice of notes, harmonies, rhythm and other musical parameters, which place the sound into a musical context. Benson has named this the Baroque or classical tradition of improvisation, where with a minute change in tone or a single addition of a tone or pitch, the performer is breaking away from the notation and is improvising, within a strict, yet open-to-interpretation, level. Gradually, Benson allows the performer to add to the written composition, and a state of shared creation and responsibility is evoked between performer and composer. Consequently, the performer becomes part of the musical tradition or notation of the composer, which has modified and changed the tradition of the original piece. Such transitions are of course part of the constant change in music, musical preferences, and context in which the music operates. However, it is this subtle change through improvisation which allows the boundaries to broaden once they are discovered. Translating these gradations from the classical to the jazz domain, or even pop domain, it becomes increasingly clear that context, as well as the ability to adjust and change preferences through tiny changes, is already an act of improvisation, meaning that we have to look at the gradations of how we improvise, rather than at improvisation as a whole. It is a constant reworking of what we know and the known way of using it. Therefore, we can confidently say that every one of us improvises, in different shades of grey and with different intentions or aspirations.

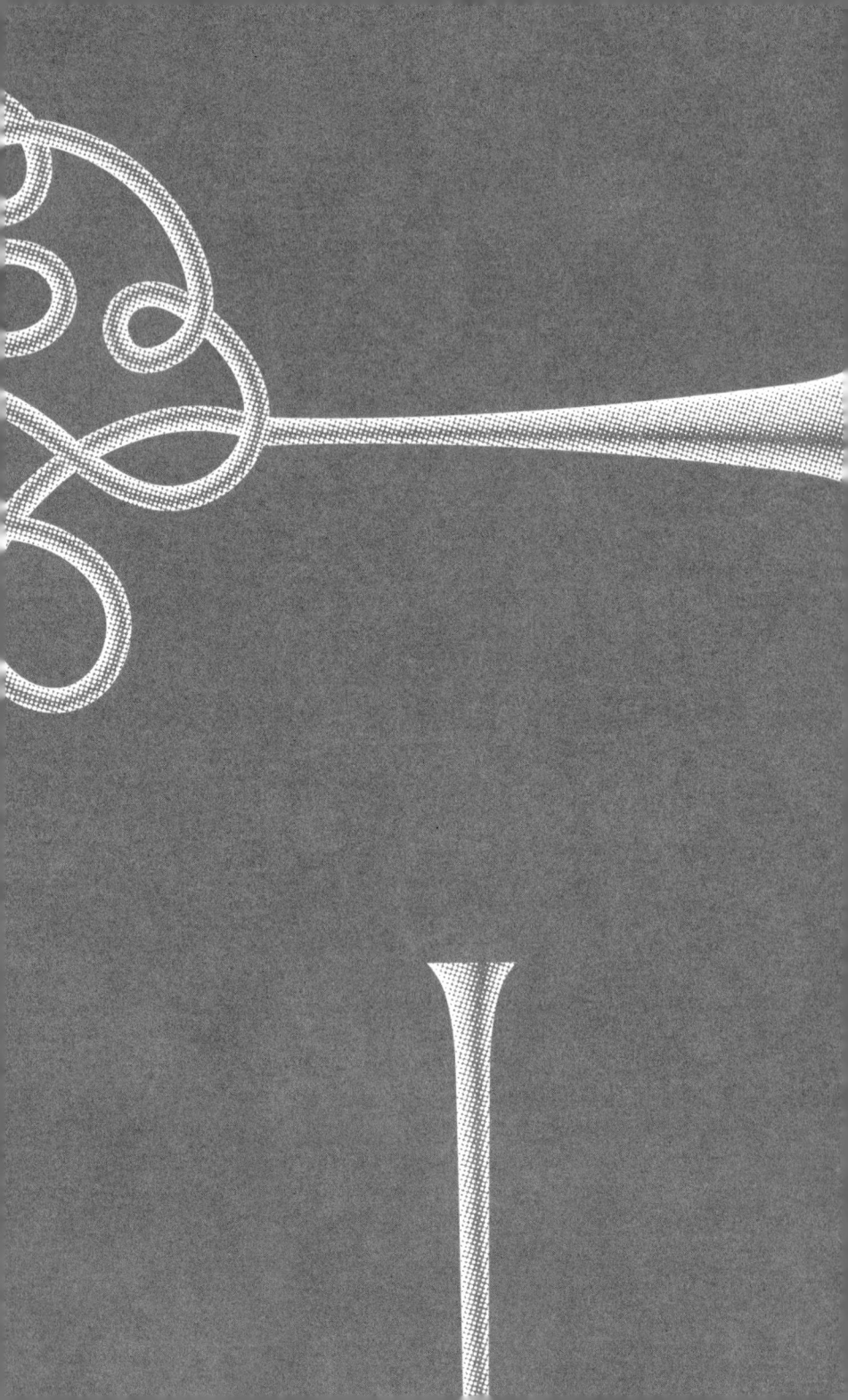

PART II

MUSIC, IMPROVISATION AND THE BRAIN

Can we consider the brain as a machine? Or is the brain more like the internet? It is rather strange that over the centuries we have always associated the brain, and the body as a whole, with machines or other physical things around us. During the Industrial Revolution the body was regarded as a combination of wheels and cogs, and today we liken it to the internet or a computer. We tend to look for answers in material things, which we have built and developed ourselves, not realising that it is these machines or networks that are built in our image, not the other way around. We therefore cannot find the answers to the working mechanism of the brain or the body in opening up the bonnet of a car—no matter how similar a modern combustion engine is to our body—or look at the vast network of servers and personal computers to explain the way our brains work. Can a computer think like a human? No, of course it cannot. It will always think differently, as it is not human. A different question altogether is can a computer imitate the way a human thinks?

With the advent of modern brain scanning, we have gained increasing insight into how the brain works. One type of brain scanning is functional magnetic resonance imaging (fMRI). The fMRI scan may be familiar through the successful doctor TV series, *House MD* and *Gray's Anatomy*. It resembles a large capsule with a magnet encircling a stretcher: clinical white for adults or playful yellow for children. A strong magnetic field is created around the person lying on the stretcher, which shows an intriguing array of biochemical and physical processes, thus gaining a glimpse into how the brain works.

Unfortunately, such technology has presented us with even more questions about the vast network of the brain and the mechanisms which guide it. Nonetheless, it allows us to study the brain during different tasks and brings us one step closer to unravelling its

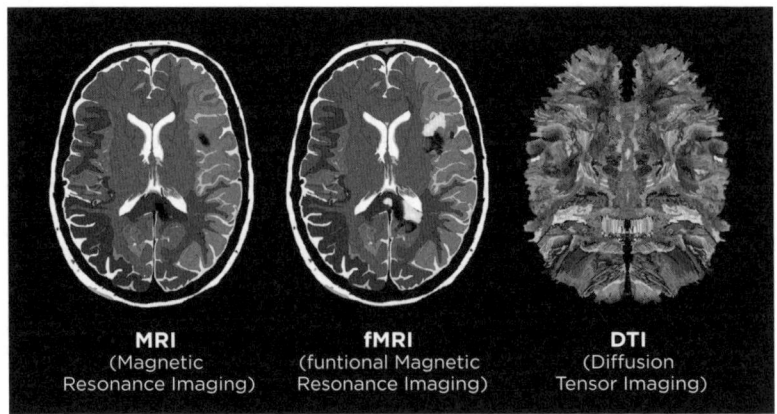

MRI
(Magnetic
Resonance Imaging)

fMRI
(funtional Magnetic
Resonance Imaging)

DTI
(Diffusion
Tensor Imaging)

workings. One crucial thing which we have learned from multiple brain scans is that everything that happens in the brain happens because of a network of areas. There is not one area solely responsible for music, or language, or our ability to calculate a mathematical problem. Such cognitive tasks require different areas and functions of the brain. Even the most basic bodily functions, such as hunger, thirst, the beating of our heart, or the inflating and deflating of our lungs, are based on networks involving different areas of the brain. These basic functions, crucial to our survival, use much simpler networks that act more in the background, meaning we do not have to be continuously aware and conscious of making our heart beat or our lungs work. They are built into our brainstem, the connection between brain and body, and comprise one of the oldest evolutionary regions in our brains. The brainstem controls many of these basic functions, which in turn are also triggered by external factors and our cognition. Imagine you are in a panic situation, or hold your breath and 'listen' to your heart and body. You will see that both the external change (holding your breath) or imagining that you are in a life-threatening situation (cognition) will alter your heart rate and breathing. Brainstem, body and the neocortex (which 'sits' on top of the brainstem) are connected to each other in more than just a physical sense.

1
EMBODIED COGNITION

The idea of a mind–body connection is as old as humanity itself. Around 400 B.C., Plato had already posed the question of whether the mind has control over the body or the body control over the mind. The French philosopher René Descartes raised the same question in his debates on 'mind–body dualism' in the seventeenth century, as did Maurice Merleau-Ponty in his book *Phenomenology of Perception* (1945). From a pragmatic perspective, reviewing all the available literature on this topic would inflate this book beyond the comprehensible or necessary. For this reason, I will not be discussing the plethora of available empirical data; instead, evidence from philosophy, neuroscience, psychology and musicology, already an abundance of data, will be used.

Embodied cognition has caused much excitement. It is the notion that to fully understand how the brain works, how cognitive processes operate, we have to acknowledge that the brain resides in a body. It uses a body to perceive the world around it and thus experiences all of its sensations through the sensory organs. These organs are important, not only because of the information they send to the brain, but also for the way in which we acquire that information and sample our world. In order to be able to experience the world around us we mostly depend on movement, which is coupled with space, which in turn is linked to time. Investigating the notion of the world without a sense of time, or more precisely, time as a superstring and reducing it to gravity alone as both physicists Albert Einstein and Stephen Hawking have researched, is surely exciting but beyond the present scope.[19] However, considering movement with all its parameters, and translating it into the way in which we experience the world, there is little we can actually do without moving our bodies. The only way the brain can communicate with the surrounding environment is through the body. Denying this and seeing the brain simply as some sort of passive sensory filter, receiving a wealth of interesting sensory information that it has to make sense of, is a false view of the role the brain actually plays.

The brain does more than just filtering and making sense of sensory input. It is *venturing out of the skull* and sampling the input, and uses the body to do this under all the imperatives that having a body implies. Embodied cognition, therefore, is about acknowledging the importance of the body. There are several different commitments and ranges to an embodied context, ranging from a lack of activity to hyperarousal. It is the actions that we perform and the feedback of these actions in the context of the world around us that allows embodied cognition to elevate the role of the brain to more than just sensory input, computing and interpretation. Let us take the ability to *see* as an example, rather than the more complex ability to hear. Active vision or active sensing makes life more complex as we have to identify, process and physically engage with the object we are seeing. When we 'learn' how to see we perceive the object, meaning we see it, but we do not know what it is. The link between seeing and knowing is therefore a physical as well as cognitive exercise. In order to understand the perceived object, we touch, taste and smell the object. We experiment with it and put it under our childish scrutiny; like putting an antique watch in a glass filled with water only to learn that it was not water resistant. If we wanted to use this experience and translate it to a computer algorithm and teach it to look, in order to identify a potentially harmful individual in an airport lobby, the algorithm would need to sample information to resolve uncertainties about what the person is doing and feeling, and what the person's next step might be, predicting each step of the person without knowing the experiences the person has had in the past. Without knowledge of the person's thoughts, it will be next to impossible to predict the person's actions, based on seeing alone. What the machine does instead is operate from a biased input of how a person looks, whether the person is trying to mask himself or move in a way that we could classify as suspicious. Therefore, it focuses only on external factors. In that sense, humans are less intelligent than such algorithms, because when we have something to hide, our body language changes—we start looking around us, feeling observed, and walk faster with smaller steps. Even our temperature changes when we are lying or hiding something. This too could be easily picked up by heat sensors in the camera. But now for the interesting bit: a compulsive liar will not flinch when telling a lie or hiding something, and thus will be able to slip through the system without being recognised, actually posing a real threat. Meanwhile, the person who has been running a fever or has a higher bodily temperature, as compared to the general average of 36.5 degrees Celsius, will be identified as suspicious. It is up to human agents to inform the algorithm to check and double check the data. Even though the algorithm does a rather good job, and is becoming better at it, if we as humans decide to just step back and let the machine do the work, something we have increasingly allowed since the advent of portable technology, trusting machines with more serious actions and not questioning them, we are empowering the machine to make choices which can have serious repercussions. We let go of the ability to look at a person from our own embodied experience, be empathetic and place ourselves into their shoes, and only then decide whether this person poses a threat. Such experiences can only be learnt during our life time and incorporate, besides cognition, behaviour and emotion, the ability to improvise and adapt to new situations. If we would judge the world as the machine algorithm does, we would reduce our brain to a computer that only perceives images of material objects outside of mind and body, thus not the associated experience of the object looking at the image or object itself. This may sound rather complex for something that we merely see. But let us take it up a notch. Let us argue that what we see is not what we actually see, like the camera, but a representation of the object in our mind with all the things that we have learnt to associate with it. We create mental representations of objects, as they are laden with experiences, emotions and memories and therefore we see representations of the object rather than the object itself, possibly clouding our judgement about them. A practical example of letting go of this notion of representationalism can be found in an intricate Victorian toy, a beautifully engineered robot that just by falling reproduces a very animate and intentional-looking motion. The robot is designed to 'fall' downhill, but it does this so gracefully that it actually looks as though it is walking. It simply walks down a shallow ramp and yet there are no controls, no electrical components. Everything happens in the body of the robot, in the carefully and elegantly crafted articulation of the bodily parts of which it is made. This is an example of a radical version of embodied cognition, radical inactivity if the body is sufficiently tuned to the environment. Here, cognition is not needed at all, and everything happens due to the coupling of the body with the environment in which it is immersed. Such an approach to embodied cognition is a radical notion and can be difficult to grasp; it reflects the philosophy of James Gibson, who has suggested that the way in which we perceive things is due to how we can act upon them, bringing us back to the interaction with objects in order to understand them. Therefore, something that can be seen is only seen by virtue of how it can be manipulated. We do not see the object but the opportunities afforded by that object, how we can manipulate it and what we can do with it, beyond the object itself. This leads to the assumption that every perceptual capability is grounded in a fundamental way by the opportunities for action that a percept affords, so we only see through the eyes of our muscles in terms of what it means for our behaviour. This phenomenon is called affordance and needs a good amount of creativity and improvisational skills.

We can also look at embodied cognition as an extension of mental cognition, translating mental information to an external body. Take, for example, the mobile phone. We think we know the telephone number that we want to call; we are maybe even convinced that our muscle memory (i.e., body) will remember when we are asked to type it in, but actually, the device knows the number and we are simply agents the device needs in order to find and activate that number. Cognitive competence has been extended into the physical world beyond our bodies. Has our cognition stopped once it has been externalised to the device? Or does cognition simply encompass more than just something that is happening in your head? It is the interaction between the mind, the body and the outside world, extending to devices and, for the completeness of argument's sake, to the meta-physical for some. It is a partnership with the environment and the ability to adapt to this environment by default—something which is key in the act of improvisation.

2
MUSIC AND THE INNER EAR

Music is a complex stimulus, engaging multiple areas and networks of the brain. This complex stimulus incorporates several elements, such as rhythm, melody, timbre, pitch and beat and therefore activates more than just one brain area. When sound frequencies or music are sent to the ear, these frequencies hit the eardrum. The eardrum moves to these waves like a speaker membrane resonates when we play sound through it. The eardrum is attached to the smallest bone in our body, the stapes, which moves like a hinge translating the movement from the eardrum to the cochlea, where this movement creates different pressure waves. These differences in pressure are sent through the cochlea to trigger thousands of little hair cells, which swivel back and forth with the movement of the liquid in the cochlea. They convert the mechanical signal to an electrical one through increases and decreases of spontaneous swings or oscillations of electrical currents in positively charged Kalium and Calcium ions. Each hair cell is responsible for a particular frequency, which we as humans can hear. By triggering these hair cells, they send the information on to the brain, where it can be interpreted as music or any other sound in the vast musical network. The stapes, therefore, translates a physical stimulus, the auditory waves, through a mechanical movement (the hinge) into a pressure wave in a closed container (the cochlea) where little hair cells are triggered to turn this movement into an electrical signal.

A External auditory canal (ear canal)
B Tympanic membrane (ear drum)
C Malleus (auditory bone)
F Incus (auditory bone)
G Stapes
J Semicircular canals
K Cochlea

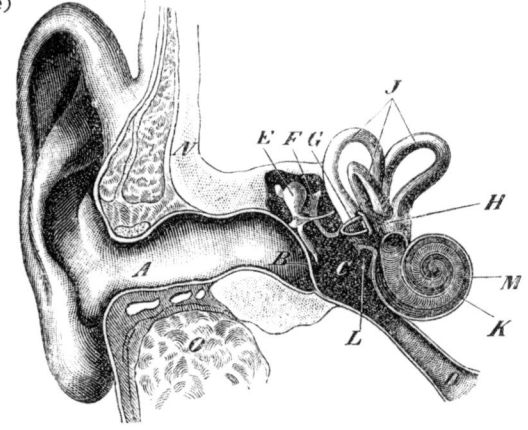

Everybody has experienced a spontaneous high beep, which lasts only a few seconds. This is different to tinnitus (a constant beep) or the noise we hear after coming back from a Rura concert, which we enjoyed without earplugs because we forgot them on our way to the venue. The spontaneous high beep is equally short-lived, however, initially becomes louder and then dissipates into silence. This beep is the last scream of a hair cell in your cochlea, the last, lonely cry, before it falls into the abyss of silence. Very dramatic, I know, but this moment marks the last time that you are hearing that particular frequency. This does not mean that you will not be able to enjoy Rura the next time you go to one of their concerts or listen to them at home. It shows that our bodies decay. Cells die and cells are generated, in our ears as well, only here we actually hear the cell dying. As we get older, we lose more hair cells, which, amongst other reasons, is why we become less sensitive to high and low frequency sounds.

3

THE THALAMUS AND THE BRAIN

Once the hair cells identify and pass the signal through to the brain, it travels via the brainstem towards the thalamus. The brainstem, you will remember, houses all vital and basic functions like heartbeat, as well as all the individual nerve fibres responsible for, amongst others, eye and head movement—one of the reasons why we move our head back and forth to the soulful beat of Beyoncé's 'Me, Myself and I'.

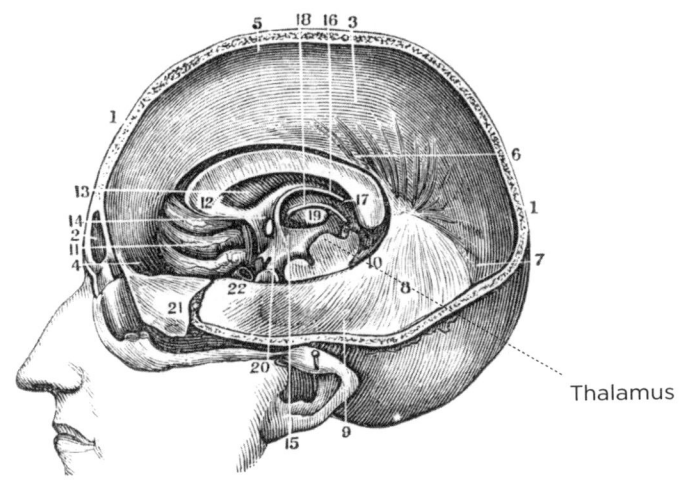

Thalamus

The thalamus is a small structure right between your ears and eyes and has been subject to multiple discussions as to its functions and role in cognition. We do not completely understand how the auditory pathways are linked to the cortex, and therefore go beyond simply relaying the signal. Thus, the question of how the thalamus contributes to the processing and perception of the incoming sound remains unanswered.

The thalamus consists of multiple nuclei, or sensory areas (receiving and sending of signals), which respond to an incoming signal. It is subdivided into specific auditory, visual, somatosensory (pressure, pain or warmth) and motor (movement) nuclei with additional nuclei sending and receiving stimuli of higher order multisensory regions, as well as so-called 'non-specific' thalamic nuclei. These non-specific nuclei create additional connections and docking points for auditory and somatosensory information. Connections between the auditory, visual, motor, somatosensory and higher order regions are made through these non-specific thalamic nuclei, creating an intriguing and complex web. The connections between the internal network of the thalamus and the vast network of the brain has been researched in animals and humans to map these different regions and networks, and the way they function—the so-called thalamo-cortical loop. The role of the thalamic pathways in the perception of music, however, has not been fully researched as of yet and therefore neither has an understanding of the whole experience of music as a complex cognitive task of tone, rhythm, beat, melody, timbre, tonal relationships, intensity and harmony, related to this thalamo-cortical loop at large. The involvement of these different components, as well as the overall experience of music, makes music a multisensory stimulus as it requires multiple brain regions and networks to be able to process it as music. As information is fed forwards and backwards between the cortex and the thalamus, the input stimulus (i.e., music) is not only identified and relayed, but in its own right 'pre-processed' by the thalamo-cortical loop, requesting cognitive, or to be more precise, executive functions to *make sense* of the incoming multisensory stimulus.

It is this "intimate and close relationship between the thalamus and the cortex" (Althusler, 1944:793), which only now is beginning to emerge in terms of the underestimated role the thalamus plays in music cognition.

> Branching input is identifiable on thalamic input, and we have seen this is a very common feature of many inputs to first order thalamic relays [...]. New questions arise about the precise content of the message that the thalamus is passing to the cortex [...]. (Sherman & Guillery, 2013:164)

> [...] and in how far there is a decoding and encoding process of the incoming musical stimulus prior to its interpretation in the cortex. (Sherman, 2016:110)

Once music has activated the thalamus and the associated networks, it continues to engage multiple brain areas, which do much more than just interpreting music. Engaging the brain with music activates responses beyond the auditory cortex in the temporal lobe, both of which are responsible for the processing of sound. Other brain networks include: the frontal lobe (our cockpit, making us who we are); areas in the temporal lobe, such as Heschl's gyrus with its function in speech production and processing; the parietal lobe, with its main functions of touch, taste and temperature; the premotor and motor cortex, dealing with movement; together with individual regions, such as the anterior cingulate cortex, the nucleus accumbens, the insula, the anterior superior temporal gyrus, the superior temporal sulcus, the hippocampus (memory), the amygdala (fight or flight), the cerebellum and the brainstem.

Overall, this network is so large that it encompasses every possible cognitive function, such as planning, working memory, long- and short-term memory, emotions and behaviour.

Neural network of involved brain areas in music; with thalamic multisensory integration at its core.

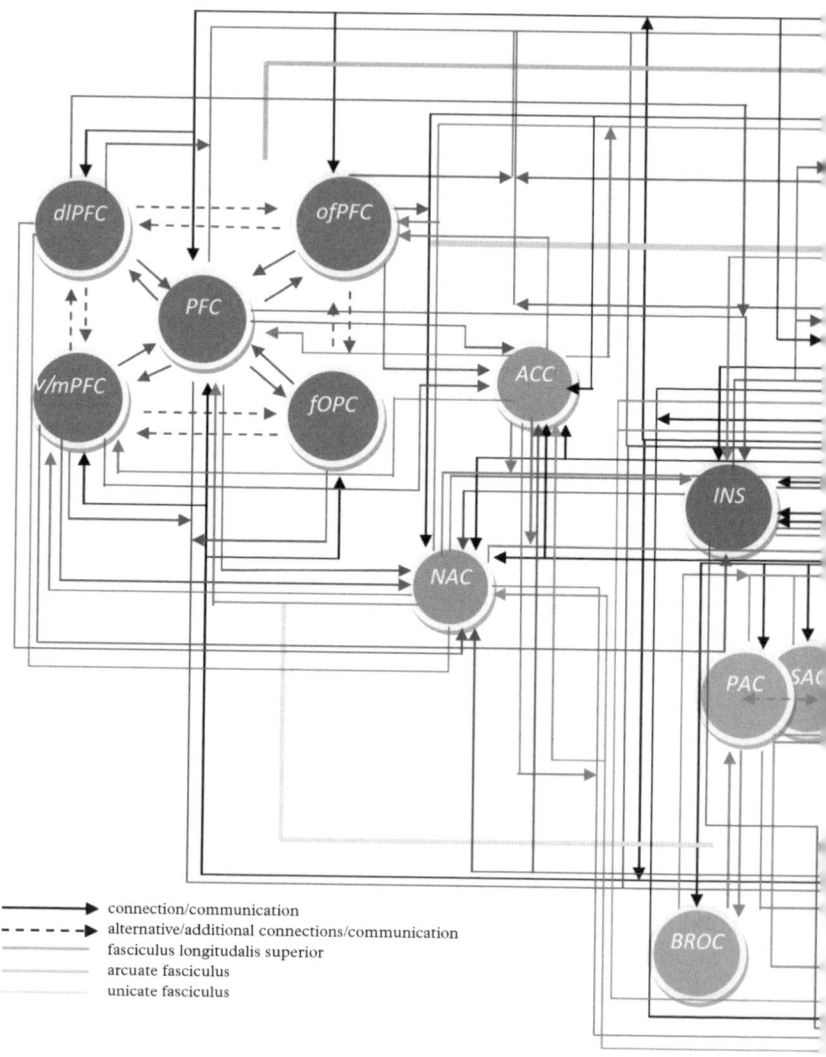

connection/communication
- - - - - alternative/additional connections/communication
fasciculus longitudalis superior
arcuate fasciculus
unicate fasciculus

Thalamic nuclei
A Auditory cortex
V Visual cortex
S Somatosensory cortex
M Premotor and motor cortex
H Higher order multisensory regions
T 'Non-specific' thalamic nuclei:
   PuM, LP, VPL, CM, CL and *MD*
   (auditory and somatosensory)

A colour version of this network map can be found on the inner back cover.

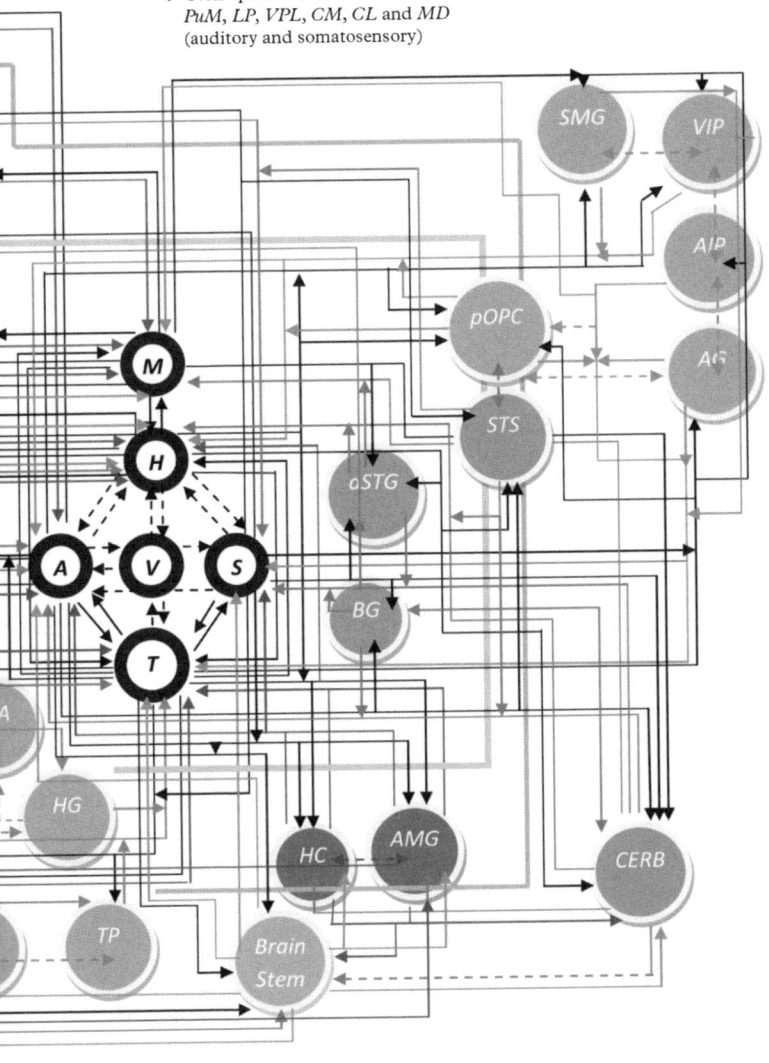

	ABBRE-VIATION	FULL	FUNCTION (WHERE APPLICABLE)
DARK BLUE THE THALAMIC NUCLEI	M	Premotor and Motor Cortex	
	H	Higher order multi-sensory regions	
	V	Visual Cortex	
	S	Somatosensory Cortex	
	A	Auditory Cortex	
	T	Non-specific thalamic nuclei	
RED FRONTAL LOBE	PFC	Prefrontal Cortex	Executive functions in interconnection with the here presented sub areas
	vmPFC	Ventromedial Prefrontal Cortex	Emotion regulation and regulation of anxiety and fear
	dlPFC	Dorsolateral Prefrontal Cortex	Decision making, e.g. improvisation
	ofPFC	Orbitofrontal Prefrontal Cortex	Decision making / emotion / reward / emotion control
	mPFC	Medial Prefrontal Cortex	Evoked autobiographical memory
	fOPC	Frontal Operculum	Cognitive process control
GREEN TEMPORAL LOBE	PAC/SAC	Primary/Secondary Auditory Cortex	Pitch decoding
	WA	Wernickes Area	Speech identification
	HG	Heschls Gyrus	Pitch interval and melody perception
	BROC	Brocas Area	Language perception / interpretation
	PLT	Planum Temporale	Timbre and spatial location of sound
	TP	Temporale Plane	Emotion/attention/ behaviour/memory

ORANGE / AQUAMARINE PARIETAL LOBE	*SMG*	Supramarginal Gyrus	Somatosensory as well as space and limb location information, and part of the Mirror Neuron System
	VIP	Ventral Interparietal area	Sensory information – visual / auditory
	AIP/AG	Anterior Interparietal area	Sensory information – sensational shape / size / orientation / visuomotor transformation of actions
	pOPC	Pariatal Opercullum	Junction of the two main fasciculi
	STS	Superior Temporal Sulcus	Sensoric pitch pattern recognition
	aSTG	Anterior superior temporal gyrus	Recognition of social cognition e.g. in improvisation / direct connection to primary auditory cortex / streams of sound recognition
	BG	Basal Ganglia	Sensoric rhythm pattern recognition / initiation of movement
BLUE MOTOR AND PRE- MOTOR CORTEX	*pMC*	Primary Motor Cortex	Execution of movement
	MC	Motor Cortex	Planning / execution / control of movement
GREY / PURPLE / AQUAMARINE	*HC*	Hippocampus	Memory function
	AMG	Amygdala	Emotion decoding
	CERB	Cerebellum	Movement / rhythm perception
	Brain Stem		Rhythm / sensory input / arousal
PURPLE / AQUAMA-RINE	*ACC*	Anterior Cingular Cortex	Regulation of activity / experience – listening / playing
	INS	Insula	Processing emotional aspects
	NAC	Nucleus Accumbens	Dopamine production

4

A BRIEF LOOK AT EMOTIONS

The study of the emotions could fill volumes. Years of research have been committed to mapping, understanding and translating emotions to human behaviour and the role they play. Looking at music and the emotions, for decades scientists have tried to understand the way in which we perceive emotions when listening to music, and most likely they will continue to do so in the years to come. Emotions play such an important role when listening to music that we cannot look at improvisation and not take emotions into consideration. Emotions are, of course, a subjective experience. The way we are made happy or sad by a piece of music is incontrovertibly linked to the different memories and associations we have encountered over the course of our lives. It is, at least from an experiential point of view, so much more than an interaction between hormones, electrical and mechanical signals, and connections in our brains. Emotions are triggered through hormones and associated memories, but how we acquire those memories, how the links are made and imprinted deeply onto our memory, is as individual as our music taste itself. The complexity of associative memory in conjunction with memories, will allow one person to cry every time they hear 'Patience' by Guns n' Roses, and smile when hearing 'Like Toy Soldiers' by Eminem. The same tunes can have the completely opposite effect on another person. Even though these experiences are subjective, we can identify certain overarching responses to music, which fuel each other, or can be seen as coherent in most people. One is the ability to regulate our emotions. We know very well which piece of music to put on when we are feeling sad, in order to become even sadder. Or which piece to play when we want to elevate our mood. Another ability we have is to boost our sports performance through music, playing Chopin's 'Nocturne No. 20' to perform better. Top sports people often play slow and laid-back music, rather than upbeat music, before a one-hundred mile run or an important competition to get *into the zone*, into the so-called *runner's high*.[20] Yet another is group dynamics and the impact our direct surroundings have on our emotions and behaviour. What we feel, what the associated emotions are, and how we present ourselves to the outside world, can be juxtapositions of emotion and behaviour; we think that we know what we feel when we express it. As an example, let us travel to Australia and the Sydney Opera House where a thousand people are gathered to listen to one of the famous fairy-tale Johan Strauss performances by André Rieu. It may not be the favourite music of each individual present, but seeing others openly weep from joy, despair or disbelief affects the whole opera house and everybody witnessing the performance. Every person present has become part of a collective experience, feeling and experiencing each other's emotions and behaving accordingly. Regardless of how we ourselves perceived that event, it would have become imprinted onto our memory as *associative memory*, a memory concomitant with our emotions, behaviour and cognition, involving the vast brain network we need to understand music, our emotions and memory. Thus, listening is more than the cognitive representation of music in our brains; it is an embodied experience which contributes to our understanding of the world around us and the ability to choose how we can interpret this multisensory stimulus. Only when we learn how to listen with our *hearts*, will we know how to listen with our brains and, in turn, be able to apply the way we experience music in different settings: at home, and in education, medicine and therapeutic interventions.

5
THE COGNITION
BEHIND THE MUSIC

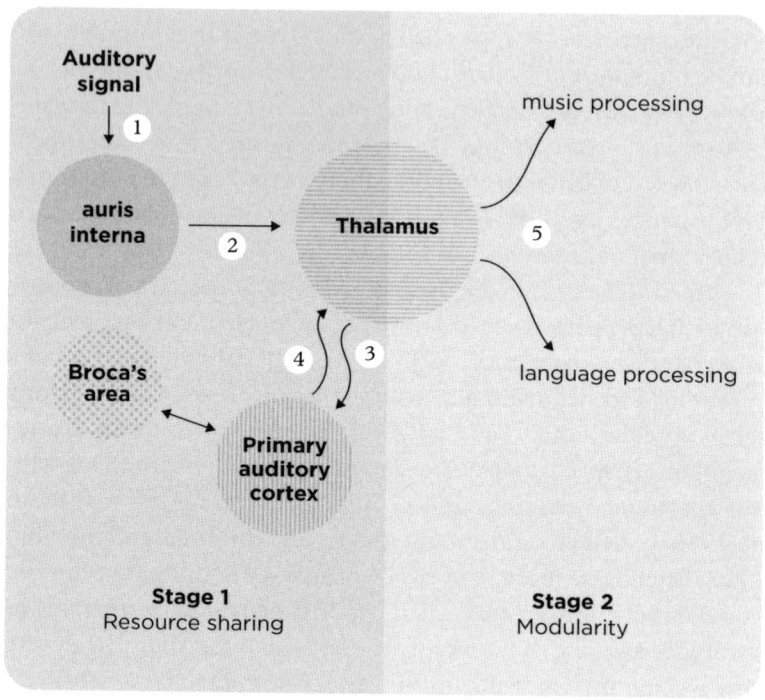

Understanding how complex music is and how it works on our brains, scientists have come up with four cognitive hypotheses—the neural identity hypothesis, the neural sharing hypothesis, the neural overlap hypothesis, and the neural dissociation hypothesis—as well as neuroscientific models, such as the arousal mood model and the plasticity model. Neuroscientists Anirud Patel and Isabella Peretz have both researched the cognition behind music. In their quest, they have devised multiple theories, two of which are still debated today. Patel, in his resource-sharing hypothesis, has argued that every piece of perceived auditory information, whether it is language or music, shares common brain areas and networks. These shared areas work together to make sense of the auditory stimulus and must have a common origin in their evolution. Peretz, on the other hand, in her modularity hypothesis has argued that auditory information must have different neural foundations, being processed in different parts of the brain. Both of these hypotheses are based on case studies and research on individuals and how they perceive and process language and music.

After analysing the theories presented by both Peretz and Patel, I would like to propose an extension to these, based on their case studies. Looking at both modularity and resource sharing, which in themselves are valid theories, I wish to suggest a combination of both based on recent knowledge about how the brain works, and how it processes information. We can argue that both Peretz and Patel's hypotheses are interlinked and can be divided into two stages: 1) resource sharing, and 2) modularity in the event of sound perception and processing (see Fig. 1). Here, the thalamus relays the signal between the necessary brain networks. In stage 1 an auditory signal (i.e., language or music) is perceived by the auris interna or inner ear, sent via the thalamus to the auditory cortex and then back to the thalamus. During this stage the brain is sharing resources in perceiving the signal in a general way. It regards the signal as auditory without interpreting it as music, language or any other sound. After the signal has reached the thalamus for further processing, the modularity hypothesis (stage 2) comes into play to finally process the signal in the different hemispheres for language, music or any other sound. In light of both hypotheses being interdependent, rather than two individual approaches, let's have a closer look at the specific functions occurring during music perception and processing. When music enters the ear, the cochlea sends this information through the thalamus, which is part of the brain stem, to the primary

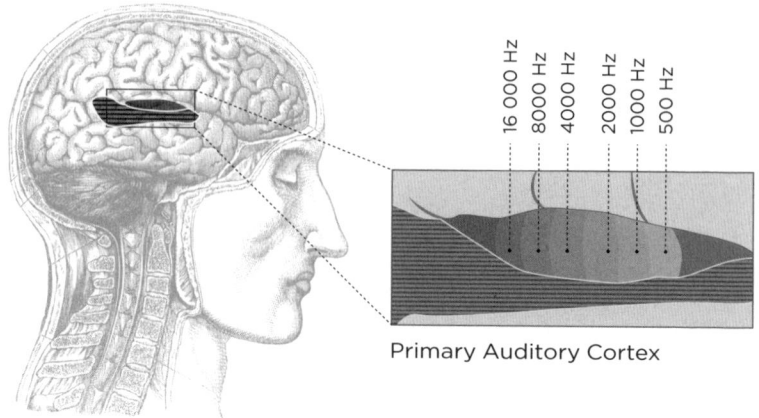

16 000 Hz
8000 Hz
4000 Hz
2000 Hz
1000 Hz
500 Hz

Primary Auditory Cortex

auditory cortex. As we already know, the cochlea is equipped with different sensory receptors, or hair cells, which vibrate according to different frequencies. These hair cells react to auditory information and generate fluid waves in the cochlea through vibrations in the conductive apparatus. To translate these vibrations into neural signals, the cochlea identifies the pressure of the fluid waves of each individual hair cell. This translation of mechanical into electrical responses is sent to the thalamus, which already serves as an initial sound processor. Neuronal pathways relay this information to the relevant parts of the brain for processing. Once the auditory cortex has identified the signal as being a set of organised frequencies or music, with layers specialised in individual frequency perception, it is sent back via the thalamus to different parts of the brain for further analysis.

Listening to and performing music is a global cerebral process, meaning that it activates the whole brain, with its different parts in turn, such as Heschl's gyrus in the temporal lobe, dealing with pitch perception (pitch intervals and melody), the planum temporale, concerned with timbre and spatial location of sound, and the anterior superior temporal gyrus, which identifies streams of sound. The processing stage, after having identified the signal in the auditory cortex, activates deeper sub cortical brain regions. The cerebellum and basal ganglia proceed with the identification of the timing circuits in order to pick the rhythm.

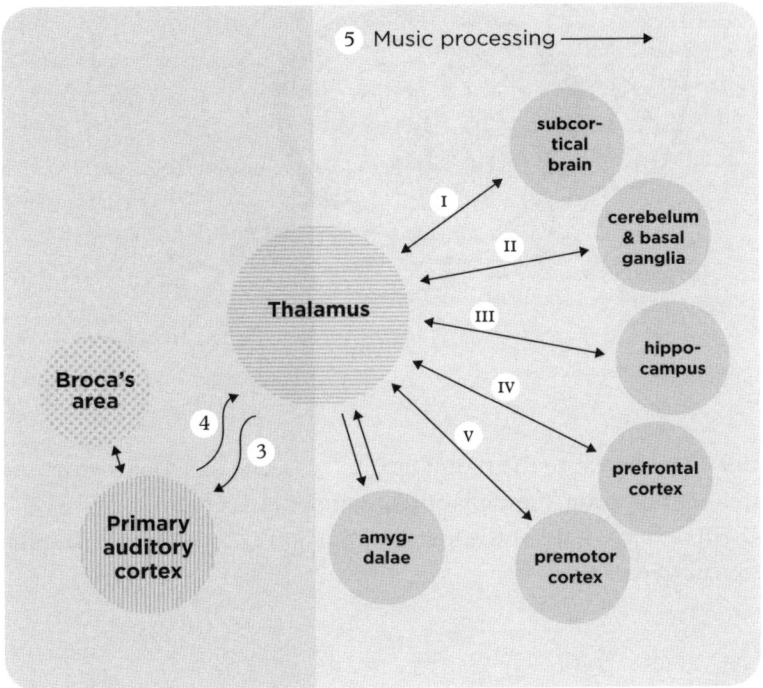

The thalamus, in communication with the amygdalae (our flight or fight response), is checking the information for danger signals, hence evoking an emotional response. The hippocampus (our hard drive) starts to compare the new signal with remembered information and sends the signal on to the prefrontal cortex, where a series of anticipations and expectations of the music are triggered. Additionally, Broca's area, which is mainly associated with the processing of language, serves as a further interpreter and finally

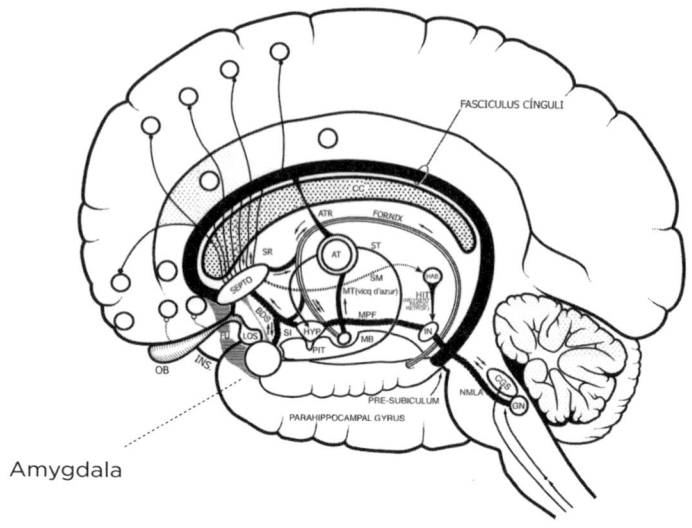

Amygdala

the signal is sent to the motor cortex, resulting in a motor response, i.e., foot tapping, dancing or playing the instrument.

All of this is happening instantly as soon as musical information is sent to our ears.

6

EXECUTIVE FUNCTIONS
AND THE BRAIN

Music and how it affects, touches and possibly influences our brain and cognitive development only reaches its full potential when understanding it within a wider context. Tracing the musical stimulus has proven to be a rollercoaster ride through the different areas of the brain, as well as emotions and behaviours. In order to

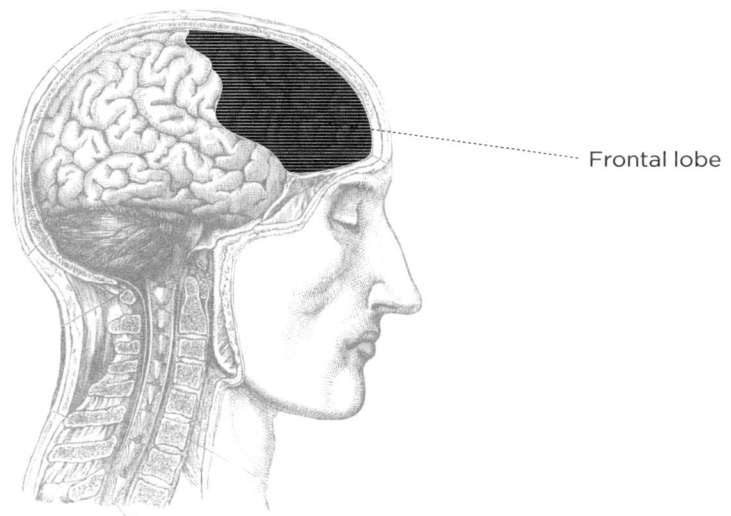

Frontal lobe

understand these connections better, let us quickly look at a set of cognitive functions, which guide our behaviour and emotions and link the different brain areas, as well as the resource sharing and modularity hypotheses—the executive functions.

These functions rule our everyday life. Whether we are trying to plan our next holiday, initiate a conversation with a friend, or inhibit our emotions, executive functions are everywhere. We are also capable of cycling and having a phone call at the same time or texting and walking through a busy street, without bumping into somebody. And if something, all of a sudden, does appear in front of our steering wheel, we are quick to break or change course, and prevent an accident. Having said this, there is no excuse whatsoever for 'multitasking' on the bike, in the car or while walking, as there are occasions when your executive functions will not work fast enough and you will cause an accident.

Yet, all of these actions require multiple executive functions which can be defined very clearly, as they translate to our everyday actions, linking cognition, behaviour and emotions together. They do so through planning, attention, working memory, empathy, motor-control, reasoning, decision making, mental flexibility, multitasking, initiation, emotion control and inhibition, and originate in our frontal lobe.

As with every function, executive functions are an elegant ballet between *on* and *off*, between the activation and deactivation of individual brain areas and networks.

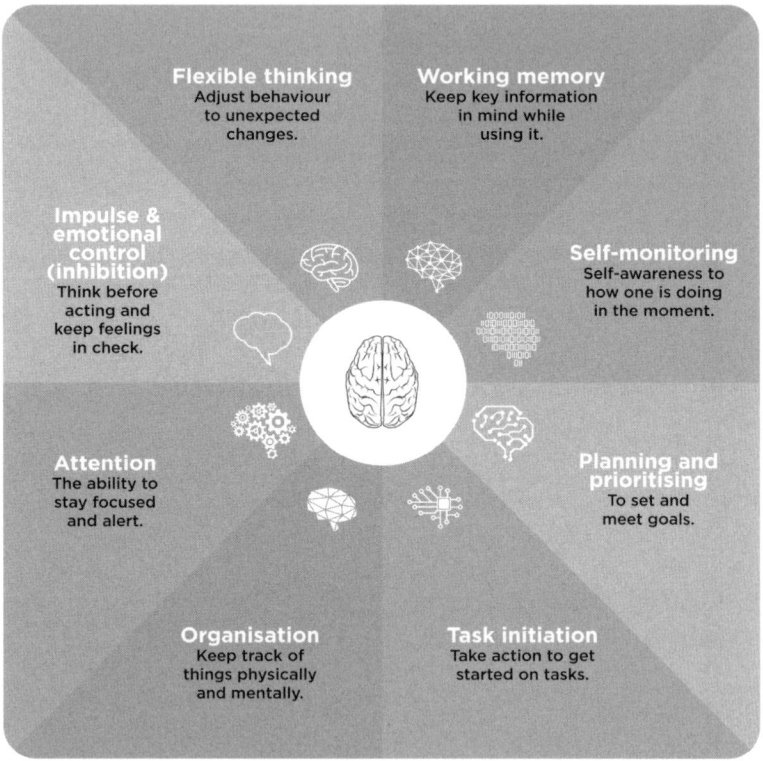

Research on the development of the human brain has indicated that it reaches its full level of maturity at around thirty years of age. This does not mean that you will not be able to develop your brain, learn new things or change ways of thinking as you age; it simply means it will take longer and is more difficult the older we get. During these early and very important years of development, the frontal lobe is one of the last areas to reach full maturity. With the prefrontal cortex being the primary seat of executive functions, one possible effect of music, be it a combination of listening, playing or improvising, is the potential to influence and benefit the development of the brain, especially the frontal lobe with its executive functions. Processing music engages long networks in the brain and overlaps with regions that are responsible for executive functions. Imagine that you are sitting in a concert hall, listening to an orchestral performance. Even though you enjoy the music, you are picturing yourself somewhere else, maybe having a drink with friends, or on a long walk to a beach café. In short, you cannot get into the groove of the music playing. You could make the decision (executive function) to stand up and walk away halfway through the trumpet part, most likely making a fool of yourself. In such a situation, your inhibition (another of those executive functions) kicks in, together with planning, emotion control and motor control. You stay seated and initiate the thought that you could just as well slip away during the interval, which will be in about ten minutes, and then nobody will notice, nor will it be socially inappropriate. Executive functions have just saved you from becoming the talk of the town as the philistine who left halfway through Mozart's 'Jupiter Symphony'.

The importance of executive functions becomes even more apparent when they are not working properly, i.e., executive dysfunctioning. Imagine if, in the above example, only one of those executive functions had not worked properly; you would have left, or made another decision, or some completely other combination of events would have taken place. Life would be very difficult indeed. We often observe executive dysfunctioning in people with neuro pathologies, meaning they have brain-related conditions, which either alter, influence or fail to activate executive functions at all. Think of people on the autistic spectrum, the elderly with a form of dementia, or people suffering from mental health issues. The dysfunctioning of only one executive function, like for example inhibition, can lead to a total overload of information, opening up all brain pathways for an incoming signal, and activating all brain areas at the same time rather than in turn: maximum overload. This overstimulation would lead to a loss in focus, distinction of emotions, remembering and learning, and initiating actions, and even to a change in our sense of touch. And this is only inhibition that is not functioning properly. Imagine now that we as *neurotypicals*, with no obvious brain-related issues and able to use different executive functions all at once with various levels of proficiency, would not be able to distinguish between our emotions or inhibit our anger. For one moment try to place yourself in such a situation, where you are not in control of your executive functions, hence, your behaviour and emotions. Maybe then it is easier to understand people with different executive dysfunctioning issues and adapt society to their needs, rather than forcing them to change to ours.

INTERMISSION

Since ancient times, music has been applied as therapy. In Greek mythology, Apollo was the god of both medicine and music. Around 550 B.C., Pythagoras demonstrated that music follows a mathematical order. He saw mathematics as the underlying principle in music which creates harmony, or the illusion of tonality. This has led to the idea that in cases of disharmony, such as illness, music could work as a therapy. This early music therapy was called 'katharsis' (emotional purification) and was primarily targeted at the soul but could also have an indirect effect on the body. Depending on what therapeutic effect Pythagoras wanted to achieve, he chose a suitable scale, melody, tempo, rhythm and instrument, still very similar to how music therapists work today. Moreover, in Ancient Greece, the philosophers Plato and Aristotle believed that music could heal the soul and Hippocrates, the father of Greek medicine, is known to have played music for his patients. In the Bible, King Saul was treated for depression by harp playing. Native peoples to America or African countries use singing and chanting as part of their healing rituals. Music therapy as a profession is deeply rooted in transdisciplinary domains, such as music, fine art, healthcare, education, psychology, clinical experience and neuroscience. Music has been an important part of everyday life for humans all over the world. Musicologist Keith Clifton has argued that music can be defined as sequences of sounds and silences that a receiver or listener organises into a meaningful shape. Thus, humans perceive 'music' if sounds are organised in a meaningful, for them, way. We make music part of ourselves and see ourselves as musical beings, whether in health or sickness. Musicality, therefore, "in all its complexity, can be defined as a natural, spontaneously developing set of traits based on and constrained by our cognitive abilities and their underlying biology. In contrast, music, in all its variety, can be defined as a social and cultural construct based on and constrained by that very musicality." (Honing, 2018: 3)

7
NEURAL PLASTICITY

It is clear how important executive functions are to our everyday life and to the perception of music. But it is not executive functions alone which make the music. As the musical stimulus is split into multiple afferent signals, something neuroscientists call multisensory levels of perception, it spreads across the brain initiating all sorts of activity in different areas. This interaction between several brain networks, with the thalamus at its centre, is needed before the signal can be interpreted by *us* as music. Our cognition is trying to make sense of what we are hearing, and in turn will find the right constellation of information processing to interpret the incoming signal as music. You can of course argue that this does not happen every time you hear music, as you are familiar with the concept of music. This is true, yet it still needs to activate all those areas in order to understand it as music; the difference is it does it much faster, due to neural plasticity.

Since the moment of conception our brain keeps developing, from cradle-to-grave so to speak. Our cells divide, the body grows, organs, blood vessels and muscles attach to bones, tendons and tissue. As our body develops, so does our brain and, as you may remember, reaches its final size at around our thirtieth birthday, with the seat of our executive functions, the prefrontal cortex, maturing last. Maybe it is not surprising that teenagers and young adults do not quite know what they want or what they should do with their lives as their frontal lobes are still developing. They simply need some more experiences to mature their executive functions. Having a biologically fully grown and mature brain at around thirty does not mean that you cannot learn new things after this time—it simply takes slightly longer to teach yourself a new language, sport or instrument. The ability to learn something new after our brain is fully grown is called neural plasticity: the ability of the brain to make new connections and take over tasks if another brain area is not capable of doing the task anymore. Think of people who have suffered a stroke and have lost the ability to speak. In many cases, it is possible to bring back a certain level of speech through music therapy. Music activates the whole brain, priming areas which were not affected by the stroke, and through training allows other areas to take over a task, like speaking, even though the language area has been damaged. Neural plasticity allows us to develop our brains without physically increasing the brain's volume and make it bigger; size does not matter. It is the ability to make new connections that makes the brain develop, without physically enlarging your brain and thus head. In light of this we can also disregard the popular myth that men are more intelligent than women because they have a bigger head and hence a bigger brain. Incidentally, females usually score higher on IQ-tests than men. Brain size does not determine whether you are intelligent, have good communication skills, or whether you are an emotional and empathetic person. It is the connections between synapses and neurons that link brain areas and create what we perceive as cognition and emotion.

With every new thing we learn, with everything that we read or see or experience, neurons are reaching out towards one another to make synaptic connections. The more we practise or read, the more synapses will connect different neurons together creating clusters of neurons, which will be activated once we perform that task again. If there are enough clusters, our brain will strengthen the connections between them making a new motorway, where the information can be quickly and readily accessed, rather than having to take less used routes to connect areas; thus, task performance is more efficient, allowing for new insights to emerge at a moment's notice. As historian and philosopher Thomas S. Kuhn has put it: "people with radical new insights are either young, or have little experience" (Kuhn, 1962: 187).

It should come as no surprise that creating new connections and expanding our brain networks requires maintenance. Let us take learning to play an instrument as an example. It is a very difficult task indeed and even an extremely gifted person will have to practise to master the instrument fully. Besides all the brain areas needed for the understanding of music, we now have to add our physical body into the equation, which will perform the task of playing the music. The younger we are the easier this connection of learning and transferring to action is, as our brains are more 'plastic' and malleable. We all know how difficult it is to break a routine once we have established it. If we want to become professional musicians, we will have to practise eight hours every day for at least ten years, and professional musicians need to maintain this discipline. However, singing or playing an instrument for most of us is not about becoming a professional musician touring the world. It is about being able to share our emotions and thoughts, or to engage with other people socially through music. It is therefore not the goal that counts but the way in which you engage with music, when you pick up the instrument and stimulate all those small neurons and synapses, teaching them to find new connections and develop the different pathways associated with music. As there is no single music network, and it relies on already existing networks overlapping with other actions, like executive functions, you will not only train your musical abilities when playing, but also all the other associated areas, which will allow for a faster functioning brain overall.

8
COGNITIVE ECONOMY

With this in mind, we can now attempt to understand the complex cognitive functions of memory with its different sub-divisions. Memory is not simply memory but is divided into, amongst others, short-term, long-term, associative, auditory, visual, working and episodic. One important concept underlying all these different forms of memory is cognitive economy. Cognitive economy helps to simplify clustering memories, so we do not have to use the whole brain network all the time when we look at or perceive something. To illustrate this point, imagine a glass. We all just thought about a different glass, whether it was a wine glass, whiskey glass, pint glass, etc. Even if we all imagined a pint glass, there are different shapes and forms to that particular glass. When we see or experience something familiar, like a glass, or the world around us, our brain creates assumptions and predictions of the world as we know it. We call this cognitive economy; this allows the brain to retrieve pre-learned information for the active support of perception, processing and production. This means that we do not need to use a large amount of energy to see the world, and the glass that is standing on the table. Only when something violates the prediction of what we are seeing, say, for example, the glass all of a sudden flips up-side-down, will we notice the difference and engage our higher cognitive functions and networks to make sense of that change. It is not only cognitive economy that is at work here. It recruits other memory functions, like working memory and short- as well as long-term memory, to make sense of what has just happened. We remember what our table looks like with everything on it, the way we left it, and its position in the room (long- and short-term memory). We then remember that we have just taken a sip of water (working memory). All of these memory functions do not need our full awareness when we have performed them. While reading, we reached out to the glass, picked it up and drank without stopping reading. Our cognitive economy has mi-nimised the cognitive strain to carry out that task as it was guided by our memory. It is of course much more complicated than this, with conscious and sub-conscious processes and yet another layer of philosophical discourse, but let us keep it simple for the sake of argument. The moment we put down the glass, the task is over, and our assumptions of the world return to normal, i.e., the glass on the table. But now we notice that somebody or something has turned the glass around, violating the assumption as well as our memory of how we put it down. Now cognitive economy goes out the window, and we focus entirely on the fact that the glass is on the table, however, up-side-down. Did we do this? No, that's absurd! Did someone else do this? No, we are alone. Your mind is focused on that result, looking for answers from your previous actions, at least from the memory of such actions, and any other possible explanation. Cognitive economy has helped us so far to create mental representations of classes of objects (the different glasses), dividing the world into classes to minimise cognitive load and thus decrease the amount of information we have to perceive, process, remember and recognise, until there is a significant change in either the classes of objects, or any information about them.

Information is 'stored' in our memory system in order to be able to better understand and react to specific objects or events. We receive a lot of stimuli, whether auditory, visual, somatosensory, olfactory, and we use our executive functions and our memory to cluster them and divide them into classes to make it easier for us the next time we see them. This clustering under cognitive economy and memory falls under the sensory register, where individual sensory inputs are recorded, analysed, interpreted and sent on to the associated brain area and network. We use these networks constantly and exchange information between networks to meet the assumptions the brain makes and compare them to what we perceive; and sometimes we just cannot figure out what has happened from memory and leave the turned over glass for what it is, a mental exercise.

9
HIERARCHICAL
ORGANISATION

The sensory register is the origin of hierarchical organisation, which quickly scans the incoming stimulus for importance. Hierarchical organisation appears to be a cognitive sub-function, allowing the most important parts of the perceived stimulus to be picked out. This triggers our associative and episodic memory system to find a matching response, which in turn can be applied during the execution of a task.

Hierarchical organisation of melody (Hansen, 2010)

Neuroscientists and linguists Fred Lehrdal and Ray Jackendoff presented one of the most thorough concepts of hierarchical organisation in the event of perceiving music in their book, *A Generative Theory of Tonal Music* (1983). Their theory is based on the so-called 'grouping' system, which is based on language analysis, and proposes that certain words in language, or melodic, rhythmic, or harmonic figures in music, have a higher importance than others. When we hear them, they help us to construct and de-construct a sentence into verb, noun, adjective, which allows us to understand the meaning of the sentence faster by identifying the most important figures in it. This also relates to reading: I am cocivnced taht you cuold raed tihs, enve though the wrods do not mkae snese. In this example, which is not an attempt to follow the footsteps of the great Dadaists of our time, the hierarchy of the individual letters in a word and the hierarchy of the words in the sentence have allowed you to simply read on without stopping and wondering what was happening. We can also apply this to music, where a listener is able to hear the music and possibly what will come next, anticipating the next chord or tone. For example, a musical phrase is written in the key of C major; therefore, C would be seen as the 'strongest' point within that musical phrase. The composition around this tonal centre will be perceived on different hierarchical levels, with the fifth (G in the scale of C) as the second highest on the scale. Other notes involved in the melody and within the scale will therefore fall under these two strong points but will nevertheless contribute to the resolution of the tonic, the C in this example. This can also be applied to rhythmical structures and further to the combination of phrases, which show higher and lower points of hierarchical groupings.

And yet, music knows so much more nuance. Discrete units like pitch and the duration of a note, or more general units like dynamics, tempo and texture, are not that easily translated into a grammatical structure of hierarchy, as they are very subjective in both performance and perception. The perception of pitch alone can be divided into pitch class, height (low or high) or the moment two or more pitches sound together. They all depend on the musical

Hierarchical organisation of a complete musical phrase (Hansen, 2010)

scale, the frequencies of the instrument used, and how the instruments are tuned. More so, the musical context and the structure of the whole piece contribute to the hierarchical organisation of sound. The same happens when applying this to chords and harmony.

Chords and harmonic structures are constructed from individual tones that have a certain stability in that chord. Using this principle, chords follow a hierarchy of stability with the tonic (I), dominant (V) and subdominant (IV)[21] as the most stable chords, satisfying our expectancy, as we know this structure from Western music. In music theory the tonic is the first tone or chord in any musical scale. They dominate the fifth, etc. The numbers therefore relate directly to the numbering of the tones within that scale. Imagine somebody asks you to play a blues solo. Even though you do not know the song, the person only has to tell you the key the song is written in and the structure of the 12-bar blues (I, IV, V, I) and you can play along.

Yet there were musicians like Karl-Heinz Stockhausen, John Zorn or Benjamin Britten who moved away from these set structures. They moved away from hierarchies as agreed on in our Western understanding of music, changing pitches, tunings and harmony, and focused on the basics of music and the aforementioned frequencies and sounds that make music. Making something new and groundbreaking is therefore not a "breakthrough but a breaking-with old ways of thinking" (Kuhn, 1962: 58).

Let us now look at Robert Burns good ol' classic 'Auld Lang Syne' and devise a little experiment we can all do at home.

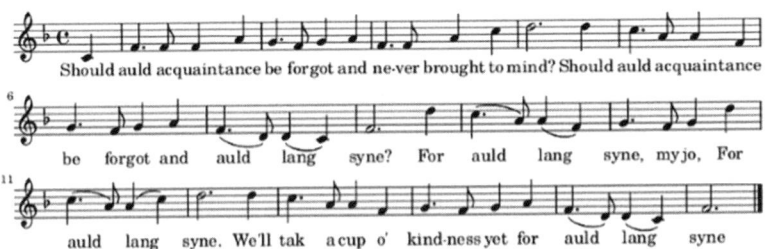

Most of us in the West can sing along to this tune, regardless of day, time or state. If we start singing it, we will follow the melodic structure and the harmony underlying it. Now ask somebody who has never heard the song before to sing along with you, for argument's sake, in the key of F Major. You make it through the first verse together. You continue, only in the second verse you stop just short of *kindness yet* and you will see that the other person will finish the verse perfectly on the F tone, satisfying all our musical need for consonance and harmony. Without knowing the tune, the person will resolve the melody as we have become used to certain structures often applied in Western music. These structures follow the tonic, dominant, subdominant tonic order, and hence a hierarchical organisation of tones, rhythms, harmony and phrases.

Carol Krumhansl and colleagues devised an experiment in the late 1970s early '80s to research exactly this phenomenon of structure, hierarchy and consonance. In their experiment, Krumhansl et al. played different descending and ascending major scales to research participants. They then asked the participants to rate the contribution of this tone to the importance of the music they were listening to. They named the tonic (I), dominant (V) and subdominant (IV) as the most important tones in any given scale, contributing to a sense of harmony and stability. They furthermore could identify the last tone in the scales in a parallel experiment when the tones were taken away and had to be sung by the participants, in a similar way to our 'Auld Lang Syne' experiment.

10
BACK TO IMPROVISATION

Try to memorise the following number: 45839485.

Now close the book and write the number down on a piece of paper. No, really close the book otherwise we will not be able to determine whether your working memory is still in good functioning order! If you managed to write down the number, then your working memory works perfectly well. If you struggled, then this may be proof that the working memory of humans in general is slowly declining, as we simply do not have to remember numbers and lists anymore to use within a 3–5 minute timeframe. Technology is partly to blame for this. We think that we know the number, but actually the device we are working with knows the number: we just know where to find it. The areas associated with working memory do still work; however, they have simply taken over other tasks and use working memory differently, due to neural plasticity.

The act of improvisation amalgamates cognitive economy and hierarchical organisation into the array of cognitive functions necessary to make it happen. So far, we have not disclosed any cognitive functions that are exclusive to musicians, or creatives, or any other specialists. Executive functions, cognitive economy and hierarchical organisation are functions we all use every day to make sense of the world around us. We access stored information and apply it to a moment, regardless of what that moment is: a conversation, looking around as we take a walk, or listening to and making music. Lawrence Zbikowski and Gregory Murphy have dived even deeper into these cognitive functions and have subdivided them into the prototype approach and the exemplar approach. The former is a collection of characteristic *attributes* or the best example of these attributes. As in the glass example, we see that it is a glass, therefore we do not have to use our brain power to identify it as a glass, but rather focus on the important part, i.e., what to put in it. A similar thing happens in improvisation. We are looking for the best characteristic to fit into the moment. Whether it should be in harmony, in tune, in line with what has been played before, or whether we will deviate completely from it and try something entirely different. We thus are able to retrieve certain musical phrases from our extensive acquired library, finding the 'best example' or best cognitive representation of that phrase suitable for the musical framework in which our musical process is taking place. At this point we are not talking about whether it sounds good or not, or whether it is what is expected from that performance. There is no aesthetic judgement, simply the interaction of cognitive functions in the moment.

The exemplar approach, on the contrary, suggests no overall collection of characteristics, which define the action, but instead individual groupings of all stored *instances* encountered in the past. Here we would search our memory for similar instances that have occurred compared to what we are trying to do in the present moment. We are not looking for individual notes, or phrases, which can be used, but rather recall instances when we improvised in the past, analysing them, cross-checking whether they would fit into the context of what we are trying to achieve, and applying them in the moment. This shows that through constant repetition neural pathways become consolidated, as well as supported, through a cognitive retrieval mechanism. These mechanisms are based on memory and how we access our memory.

Expanding on this idea, Richard Atkinson and Richard Shiffrin proposed a memory model, which today still forms the basis of how basic memory—if there is such a thing as a basic or simple cognitive function—works in the brain. Their model has three stages of processing: the sensory register, working or short-term memory, and long-term memory. Taking together what we know about how we can learn to improvise, either copying the master directly, transcribing, or through practise and experimentation, we can follow the Atkinson and Shiffrin model step by step: the 'novice' perceives the music or any other stimulus and records it in the sensory register, which is the origin of hierarchical organisation. Here, the sensory register performs a quick scan for importance and pre-processes the music, which is then sent to the working or short-term memory. At this stage, the main *coding*, *rehearsal* and *recoding processes* take place. The information is given a label and can be connected to other already known things (cognitive economy), and can be applied and linked to existing concepts and instances prototyping and exemplifying the incoming input, rehearsing it in our mind. It allows for the information to be stored in the short-term memory. The more we rehearse what we accumulate in our short-term memory when learning, the more we pave the way to our long-term memory. Once the information has been transferred to our long-term memory, our brain can further process and store the information and is later able to recall this information when necessary.

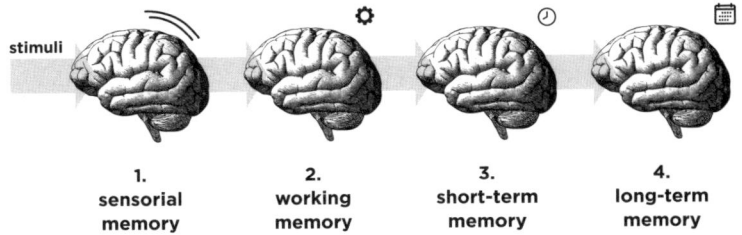

stimuli

| 1. | 2. | 3. | 4. |
| sensorial memory | working memory | short-term memory | long-term memory |

When learning music and how to improvise, we therefore add musical phrases and occurrences to our short- and long-term memory and rehearse these repeatedly, so they can become part of our sonic library. We are building and expanding our own mental music collection and the instances when and how we can use it, which is combining both the prototype and exemplar approaches. Through this constant repetition process the acquired knowledge becomes part of the episodic auditory memory, which is yet another recollection and retrieval system of the 'what, where and when' involving the long-term memory. It does not require specific training and mostly happens automatically, based on triggers from our surroundings. Due to our automatic recollection and retrieval mechanisms and their importance to our cognition, the term 'subconscious' can, in a broad sense, be connected to the term automatic. The human mind has little influence on what is stored in the subconscious. However, through constant repetition we can incorporate certain actions or even movements into a subconscious representation of that action, and consequently these actions become automatic recollection and retrieval processes. This explanation is very simplified, as a full discussion of subconscious processes is a book in itself and has so many layers that it would muddy the waters of improvisation here. In the case of improvisation, the mind has already 'remembered' the framework and structures of improvisational methods and can therefore 'automatically' apply these to a new event through episodic auditory memory, short- and long-term memory and cognitive economy. Once properly learned, a pattern will remain stored in our memory and, as Bernard Hall has put it, will be "[…] like an electrical field, holding and forming anything entering its sphere of influence. Acquired information is so basic and so fundamental that it is almost inevitably equated with the self, and its patterns are automatic and totally out of awareness." (Hall, 1999: 154)

★

In brain research, and through fMRI studies of the auditory processing of music and improvisation, scientists have shown that when we play or listen to music, and especially when we improvise, we rely on our memory as well as all the other areas necessary to this process, especially areas in the prefrontal cortex. What we do not know quite yet is which areas of the hippocampus are activated during memory retrieval when it comes to music, as music is such a complex input stimulus.

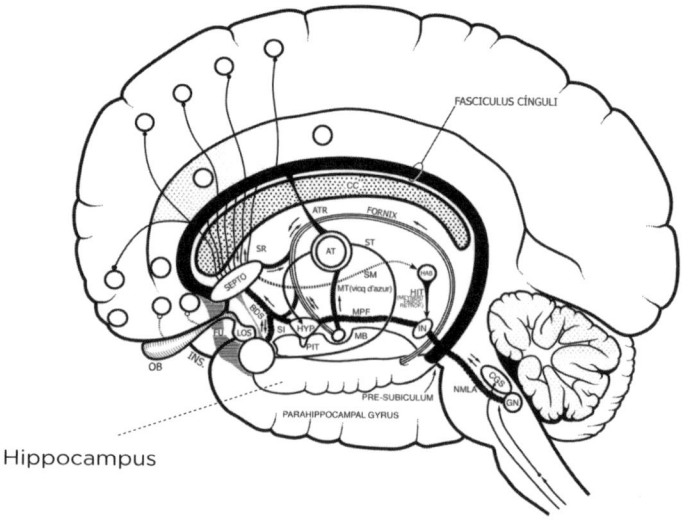

The ability to store and retrieve context-rich information depends on the connections to and from the hippocampus, how these are interlinked in the hippocampus and associated areas, and for what reason they are retrieved. Looking at episodic auditory memory, scientists have shown that there is an increase in direct connections between the auditory association areas of the parahippocampal region and the prefrontal cortex. Storage and retrieval, therefore, can only happen on a multimodal level, where direct connections between the auditory areas and the prefrontal cortex are linked to areas associated with memory, as well as emotion and behaviour. This interaction allows a direct retrieval of information in the event of prefrontal cortex activation, which again is an example of saving brain energy when we have to perform in the moment. It will not take the long way around in order to find the right representation but will base its choice on what it knows and has learned. These actions happen in tenths of seconds and require a fast-moving mind. Although working memory plays a crucial role as well, its part during the actual performance still seems unclear. Working memory is one stage in the human learning process of acquiring new information, being responsible for coding, rehearsal and recoding, and originates in different parts of the prefrontal cortex. Working memory allows the human mind to maintain information briefly in an active state. Sometimes we keep information active until we actively use it, as when we hold on to a phone number until we dial it. Do you still remember the number from the beginning of this section? Yes? Congratulations, you have made it to stage two, and it is in your short-term memory—for now. When we improvise, the sensory register, being the first stage in the memory system, will search for stable events in music. This initial search or scan allows for the perception of points of hierarchical stability, which appear to be an important first step of precoding of the input signal. Through this recognition process, the sensory register is identifying stable musical points and, based on this judgement, is evoking a response in the episodic auditory memory. Stable events in music are similar events stored in our memory. Therefore, hierarchies in the music trigger previously learned phrases and structures, which correspond to our musical knowledge. Arguing that hierarchical organisation is a triggering system of cognitive economy, human cognition must have already created relationships to hierarchal stable sounds through the precoding process in the sensory register. This makes sense as we are constantly building a musical or sonic library, every time we listen or play. These processes do not only happen when we listen. It is the different networks and the complexity of the brain that make this possible. It is not the music that trains the brain to perform these tasks, it is the brain that allows us to understand the combination of waves and frequencies as music. Hierarchical organisation analyses the music based on existing knowledge to find the best representation for a performance event.

Musical events, however, are not only processed in terms of hierarchic stability in the sensory register. We also must take melodic contour, which allows the listener to discriminate between the shape of the melody's 'ups and downs', into account. This means that an improvisation within an atonal context will rely on the contour of the musical line. Atonal music is much more difficult to listen to as it violates our expectations of order and harmony, as well as predictability. Like in 'Auld Lang Syne', we thrive on predictable sounds and sequences. We understand them. Atonal music is more complex, moving from left to right, keeping us engaged and cognitively active for longer periods of time—a full body workout for the brain. Nonetheless, the perception of musical contour, tonal or atonal, is part of hierarchical organisation. In an atonal context, however, it would be arduous to find a stable hierarchy in tone, chord or pitch. We will look for whole phrases to assign hierarchical order. This would consequently trigger memories based on these hierarchies of musical phrases.

We now understand that hierarchical organisation triggers certain episodic musical memories. The following example will bring the above-mentioned factors to the fore. My time as a jazz musician has shown me that when we experience music, we first perceive the musical context around us. Based on this framework, we pick out either tonal/chord/harmonic hierarchies or phrase hierarchies, which trigger an appropriate episodic auditory memory response. This response finds the best representation in the moment and thus combines suitable known structures by applying the concept of cognitive economy (prototype versus exemplar approach). Finally, this results in a musical experience or production. We therefore base our musical experience on the musical baggage that we have accumulated during our lifetime. A neonate will naturally have a much smaller musical library than someone aged eighty years old; this library allows for different applications in different contexts. Understanding the musical experience and its application is thus based not only on our human ability to perceive, process and make music, but also on the created and associated memories and emotions we have with the different sounds and pieces of music. Hence, listening is more than the cognitive representation of music in our brains; it is an embodied experience which contributes to our understanding of the world around us and the ability to choose how we can interpret this multisensory stimulus.

11
THE BEAUTY AND SIMPLICITY
OF THE DORSOLATERAL
PREFRONTAL CORTEX

We can now take a step backwards and focus on a specific region in the brain: the dorsolateral prefrontal cortex (DLPFC).

The DLPFC is a small area in the frontal part of the brain and is represented in both the left and right hemispheres. The main function of the DLPFC is decision making, which as we know is one of the executive functions. This brain area has the task of switching itself *on* in order to make a particular decision, before taking a step backwards and switching itself *off* after the decision is made and sent on for further processing. This area, however, needs information in order to be able to make a decision. It is of course a much wider and greater network which is involved in decision making; however, the DLPFC receives information and depending on the context in which we find ourselves, as well as the amount and quality of the information, it will open pathways to allow the information through, to become a decision. This relaying, or *on* and *off* positions of the dorsolateral prefrontal cortex, happens extremely fast. The reason for this speed is twofold; on the one hand, we need to be able to make decisions in split seconds, as they determine our actions and the way we navigate through the world. On the other, not all the information has to be digested before a decision is made, as we have seen through the concepts of cognitive economy, hierarchical organisation and executive functioning. Information is recruited from our behaviour, embodiment, emotions, and the aforementioned cognitive tasks, to make an informed choice in

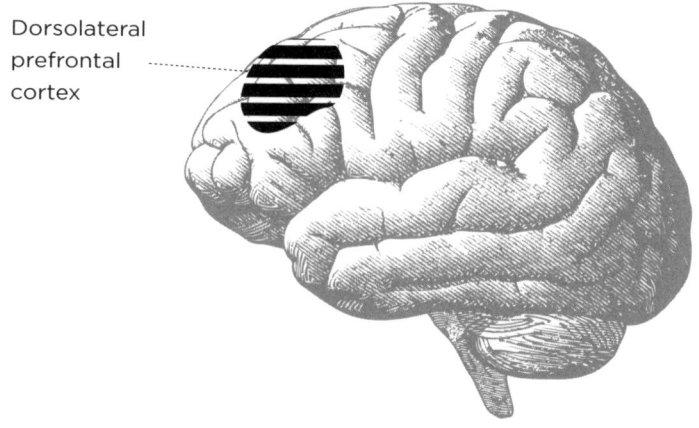

Dorsolateral
prefrontal
cortex

the moment. Musicking, and especially improvising, is based on these informed choices and they allow us to function within a context. We need to choose from context-related information in an improvisation, to either violate or satisfy the assumptions which we make and perceive in the world around us. We choose, or at least we think that we are choosing, phrases, notes, chords, or words and sentences to communicate with the outside world. We rely on our memory, and our musical or language library and the DLPFC to make the correct choice in that moment. We test these decisions through our embodied cognition and the reaction of a possible other, and judge whether we can continue with a certain line of thought, musical phrasing or conversation. If we are not stopped or end up in a verbal cul-de-sac, we will continue until we change topic. For all these acts, the DLPFC supports us in taking the path we want to pursue. Interestingly, during the actual improvisation, this decision-making area is momentarily switched *off* in order to allow unfiltered and uninterpreted information through. Neuroscientists Charles Limb and Allen Braun have shown in their research that multiple areas are active in the frontal and prefrontal areas during improvisation. Brain activity is never a constant state. What we mean by this is that the brain usually does not perform in either state of activity or de-activity. It is the delicate balance and interaction between different brain areas and networks that enables and disables information streams; yet another reason why our brain performs all those marvellous tasks with less energy than a forty watt light bulb. During this elegant ballet of selecting and clearing, the DLPFC constantly switches between the *on* and *off* state; however, the actual moment of improvisation is a deactivation state. While in *off* mode, the other involved brain areas are activated to process the information further. It appears that the DLPFC accumulates the information, decides on pre-learned and existing pathways and while switched off allows this information to proceed for further processing. There is, however, a minute moment in-between the *on* and *off* state where the DLPFC is neither active nor inactive. The activation of all involved brain areas allows us to actually play our instrument or sing in order to understand the harmonic context. The actual moment between these stages is the birth of the *creatio ex nihilo*, the creation of something new in the spur of the moment, the act of improvisation and creativity. Additional brain networks are recruited, linking the frontal lobe with areas in the limbic system. The amygdala with its flight or fight response is activated, triggering memory, as well as associations with the perceived and the played. We see, smell, hear and feel the music and the decision made, which propels us forwards to take the next move. We engage our bodies, and through embodied cognition we understand and reflect our actions in the world and the world, in turn, reflects back on us, while our parietal and temporal lobes work in parallel to stimulate the improvisation even further. The whole brain network lights up and dims in an elegant dance of enabling, inhibiting, remembering and disabling. All of these pathways have such a strong evolutionary connection that information is automatically recalled and a suppressed DLPFC no longer regulates the contents of conscious information, but allows unfiltered and random thoughts and sensations to emerge—the *creatio ex nihilo*, the moment between the *on* or *off* state. This happens a thousand times per second during the whole course of the act of improvisation.

12

IMPROVISATION COMES
WITH RESPONSIBILITY

Our brains desire structure; or do we as human beings desire structure as we have learnt how to thrive on it? At the end of the day, is it we who are masters over matter, and not our matter which is masters over us? Disappointing as it may be, this *Grundsatzdiscusion* cannot be answered in a mere reflection on improvisation, creativity and the effects of music on the brain. It does, however, give us an interesting insight into how our brain works. On the one hand, it balances between states of activity and inactivity, between enabling and disabling pathways. On the other, it allows for momentary and unguarded junctures, which provide unprecedented depths to our subconscious and automated improvising mind.

Improvisation comes with responsibility; therefore, it needs cognitive functions such as cognitive economy, hierarchical organisation and executive functions. It relies on our memory and what we remember in certain contexts, in order to simplify the world around us. We are dependent on our neural networks connecting different brain areas, which are in turn necessary to understand what we are doing, in what context we are performing, in which socio-cultural environment we are performing, and how we can judge our actions and reflect on them in the light of past and current occurrences. Music, and more so improvisation, activates the whole brain. Our ability to improvise, regardless of musicality or otherwise, is our innate ability to perform in states in-between activity and inactivity of brain function. It is the moment between pressing the light switch, the signal travelling at 670,616,629,3899 mph (or 1,079,252,848,7999 km/h) and the light actually turning on. Quantum physics has observed this phenomenon for around a hundred years: the moment of simultaneous moments, or the moment between occurrences. Erwin Schrödinger has described this conundrum in his famous thought experiment.[22] A hypothetical cat is unobserved in a closed box. Before the box is opened the cat can be considered both alive and dead at the same time. Its fate is linked to a random subatomic event that may or may not occur. That split-second moment between on and off, between alive and dead, is the moment of the actual act of improvisation. This *creatio ex nihilo* is based on pre-existing brain networks which we share and use. We recruit different brain areas, all of which have additional everyday functions other than the perception and processing of music and improvisation. We rely on our neural blueprint that is informed by our biology. Even though the way our brains communicate, connect information, or reach a conclusion varies per person, we all trust our neural networks and brain areas to do the job.

If our neural networks can already improvise, then you can too. We have only forgotten how to consciously access this ability.

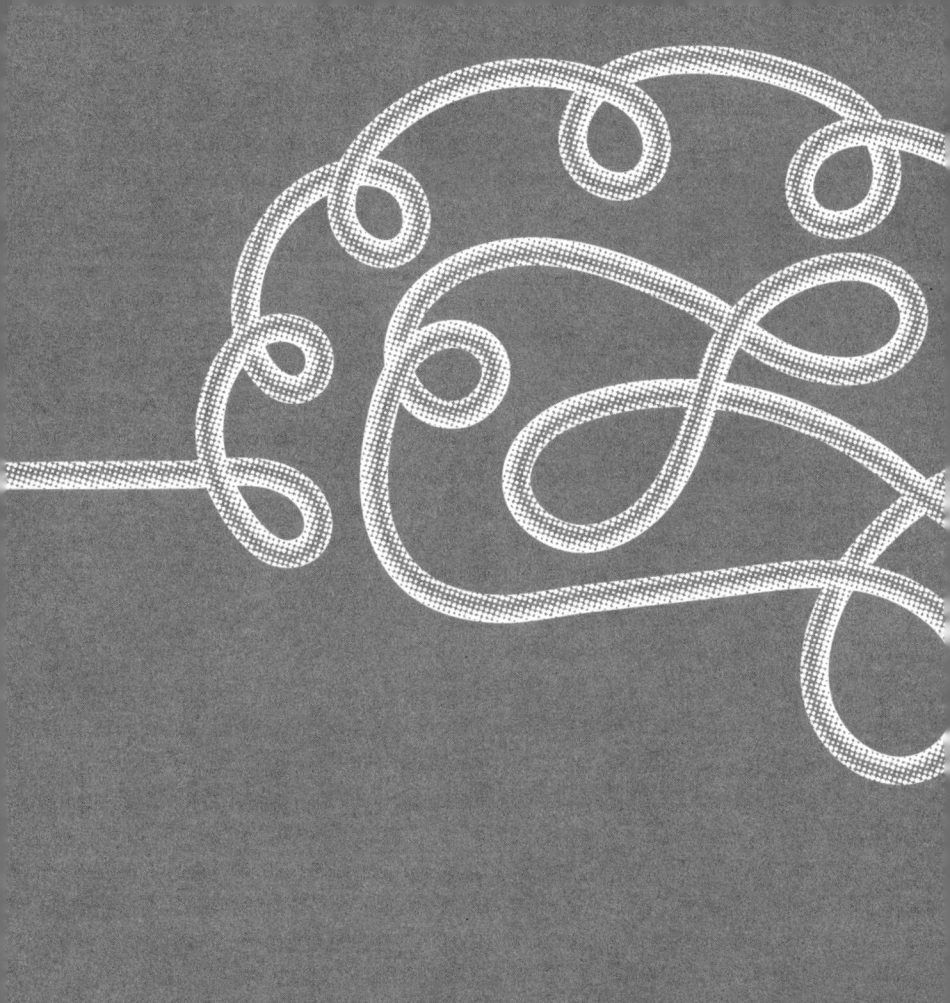

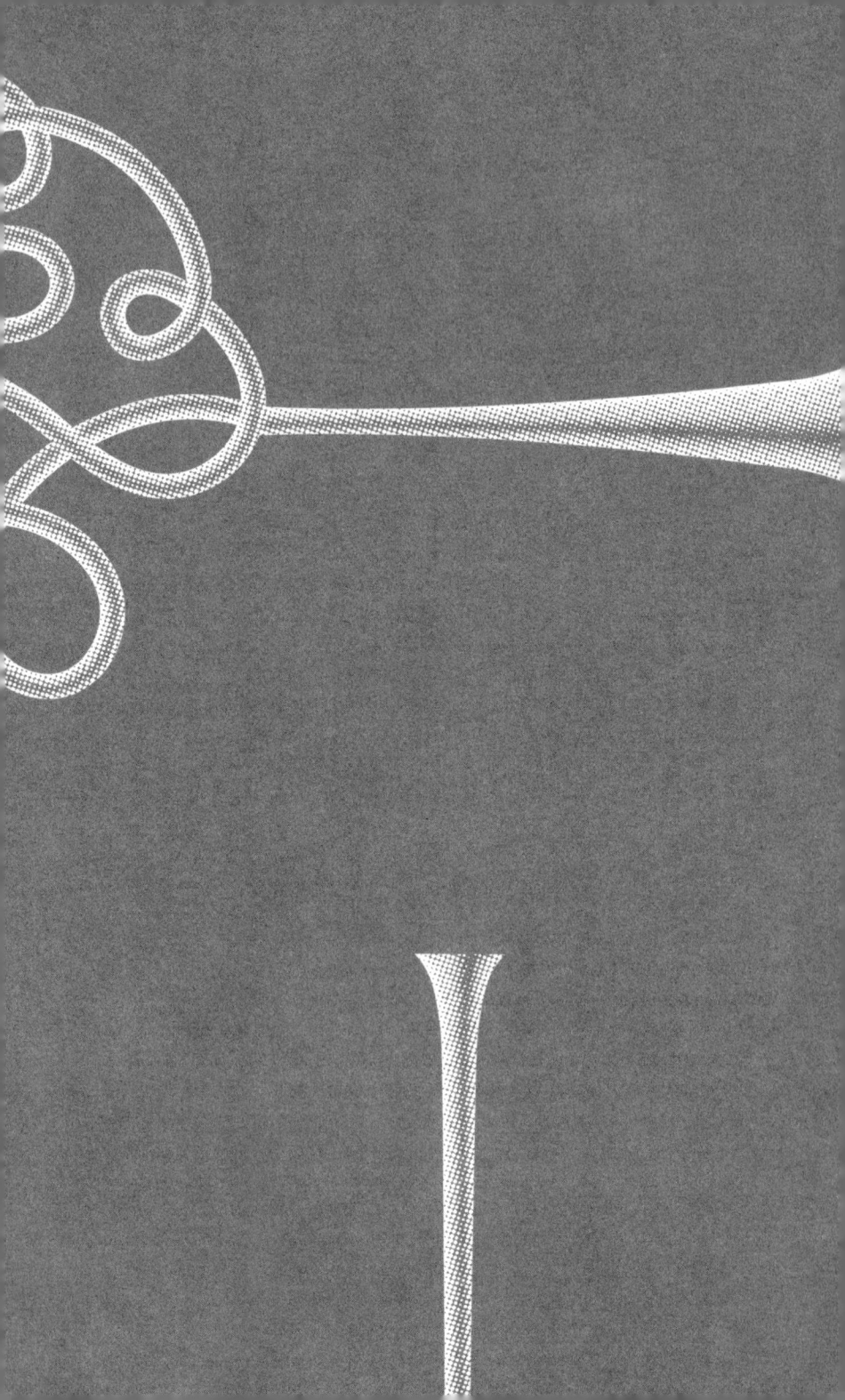

PART III

THE SECRET OF IMPROVISATION

1
ENTROPY

Every few years we discover that the brain is much more than simply an interpretation station. There is more to cognition, which translates through behaviour and emotions into the outside world and then, in turn, informs our cognition. Our mind and body search for balance, for an equilibrium in the physical world. As we have seen with embodied cognition, we project our actions into our environment; these become the world's way of perceiving us and, in turn, behaviour is adjusted accordingly. There is an elegant symmetry in these two forms of behaviour, where one action is not juxtaposed to the other but both actions mutually feed each other as we act upon the world and the world acts upon us. It is our desire to break away from chaos and find order in everything we are, perceive or process, just as we seek chaos in order. Entropy is nature's tendency to let everything fall into chaos. In other words, according to a common understanding, entropy at the most fundamental level is a measure of the value probability of particular distributions of states, cells or networks. For example: how many neurons or synapses are there and how many more need to be added to perform a task?

Neurons are cells, which make up our whole brain, and are even found in our body, such as around our blood vessels or attached to our muscles. They are triggered by electrical signals, and to a certain extent process part of the incoming signal, create a firing pattern and, if necessary, forward the signal to the next set of neurons, with each set having a unique firing pattern.

This pattern could be seen as the individual voice of that particular type of neurons with its own 'frequency'. These could be five short bursts (ta ta ta ta ta) or five short and two long bursts (ta ta ta ta ta taaa taaa), and so forth. Depending on the type of neuron, it will always fire at the same rate when stimulated. Additionally, when

Neurogenesis (Washbourne, 2009)

different groups of neurons are connected with each other, they will also be stimulated together. As neuroscientist Donald Hebb said: "Neurons that wire and neurons that fire"[23] (Hebb, 1949). To be connected, however, neurons branch out to make the connections, whether they have long axonal arms or short ones, each neuron connecting to another through synapses. These champignon-like bulges sit on the axonal arms of each neuron. There can be hundreds of them on one axonal arm, trying to make a connection between two neurons. Once a connection is made, synapses exchange electro-chemical information, with one end the sender and the other the receiver. If the information that is sent matches the port of the receiver, the electrical signal can travel onwards. Synapses exchange chemical particles, each having its own particular shape, being round, square, triangular or any other geometrical form. The sending synapse sends a 'round' particle towards the receiving end, and if the receiver accepts 'round' particles, then the signal is transmitted, hence electro-chemical. These tiny communicators are crucial in the communication of signals between neurons, thus, between brains areas, and make up part of the huge brain network we cultivate from birth.

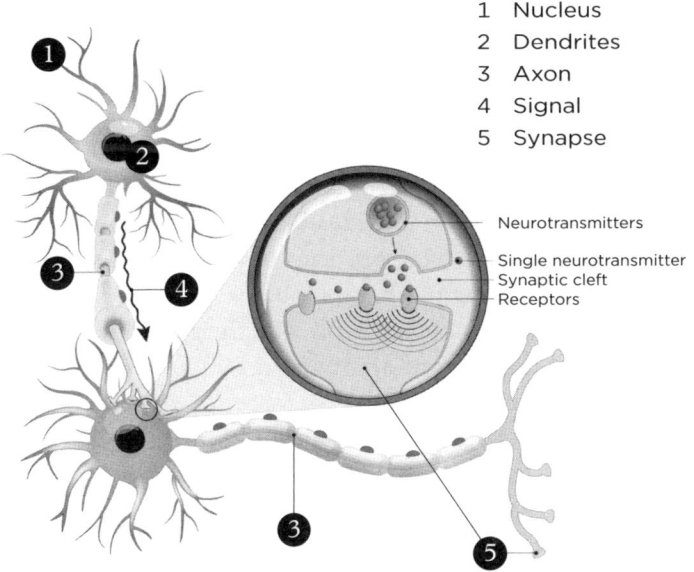

1 Nucleus
2 Dendrites
3 Axon
4 Signal
5 Synapse

Neurotransmitters

Single neurotransmitter
Synaptic cleft
Receptors

How many neurons or synapses are needed to perform a task? This is not a question with a simple numerical answer, such as how many eggs do we need to make the perfect Victorian sponge. It is not so much a precise number, but a more general estimate that allows for a possible answer. With fewer neurons, synapses and networks and therefore fewer 'degrees of freedom', which is the way the cells and networks can communicate with each other, the entropy gets smaller and can even arrive at zero. It is precisely within this 'chaos' that the interaction between our bodies and the world can occur. It is an exchange of space, where the assumptions of cognition do not hold and are replaced by *experiencing*. Chaos, in this sense, is not negative; rather, it is something that is out of order or fits into a frame and is closely related to the creation of something new and embodied—an experience that is immersive from both the world's as well as the body's point of view. There is reason to believe that the transition from order to disorder, which happens in the interaction between neurons, synapses and networks, and especially between *on* or *off* states of networks, is where creativity and thus improvisation can emerge. As Albert Einstein has famously said, "if a cluttered desk is a sign of a cluttered mind, of what, then, is an empty desk a sign of?" (no date).[24]

Translating this to music, and the way in which we listen to and make music, we experience it outside of our brain's urge to apply structure or order. Considering music as physical, with its waves and frequencies, including the building blocks of music such as melody, rhythm, harmony and so forth, and their possible effects on our brains and bodies, our attempts to structure music will always be counteracted by the physical forces of entropy, which wish to create chaos. As much as we want structure, there is always the other side of the coin, which is nature's pull of disorder. At the same time, creation can be seen as chaos. It is this intricate dance, this elegant balance between structure and chaos, where our actions can influence the behaviour of the world and vice versa. Thus, we experience full non-Newtonian *gravity*, where music and the way we understand music does not imply fall, but floating freely through a shared embodiment of our extended cognitive, behavioural and emotional bodies and the outside world we inhabit.

We therefore have to communicate with the outside world, where our ideas and assumptions, as well as cognitive capabilities, model what we are physically capable of doing. Experiencing music is more than its perception and processing; it is the desire to plant our bodies in the position to approach music, which in turn is the reflection of the world towards this desire, modelling the circumstances around us to experience the music in the best possible way. The interaction between perception and experience, where we attune to the urge to listen to music, to move to music, once it has travelled past the different nerve cells in the brainstem into our cortex and back to the body again, is the acknowledgment of our own embodied actions as they are perceived by us, others, and the world. The notion of embodied cognition in the experience of music as a whole, therefore, is an interceptive influence that complements the perceptual inference or synthesis of our inner experience (i.e., cognition, emotion and behaviour), and actions and reflections from outer experiences, operating between order and disorder. This applies beyond the visual or auditory and extends to the internal organism with heart rate, blood pressure, oxygen saturation and 'gut feeling', all of which add to the understanding and notion of embodied cognition. Experiencing a *rave*, a live performance, or a *mosh pit* translates to the entropic space, where chaos is induced from the outside world onto our order-seeking understanding of music, thus allowing us to be immersed within it: the ultimate reaction of the world to our actions.

2
ACTIVE AND PASSIVE LISTENING

"How are we going to make sense out of this?"[25]
(Holland, 1969)

So far we have focused on a brief history of music and improvisation and how we acquire the ability to improvise. Furthermore, we have looked at various cognitive processes which allow us to improvise. We engage our entire brain when we listen to or play music, and even more so when we improvise. It is a vast network of areas, which are constantly exchanging information in the trinity of emotion, cognition and behaviour.

Our ability to improvise reaches beyond music. We improvise every day, whether during a conversation, while shopping, navigating our bikes through a busy street, or making dinner. Our neural networks have prepared for this throughout our evolution and have left a significant mark on our neural fingerprint. Saying that we are not able to improvise would be like saying that we are not able to think and act. Musical improvisation may differ only in the 'language' used. Whether using words or musical phrases, overlapping brain areas and networks are activated, recruiting cognitive functions such as cognitive economy, hierarchical organisation and executive functioning, as well as long- and short-term memory, and working, associative and episodic auditory memory. Add a pinch of emotion and this all boils down to an intricate network of abilities beyond the kaleidoscope of music. Let us dig a little deeper into the synthesis of emotion, behaviour and cognition.

To be able to improvise, we need four stages of interaction with music: passive listening, active listening, playing music and, finally, improvisation. We need all four to comprehend and, even more so, engage with music, without a second thought, as our brain networks have learned the ability to listen, play and improvise. Passive listening is the ability to hear something in the background, while being actively engaged in a different activity. We are perfectly capable of having a conversation in a restaurant while there is music playing in the background. We can hear the music but it does not really interfere with our conversation. We do not realise that the tune, or even the genre, has changed as we are focused on the conversation. Our brains are well capable of distinguishing between the different sensory impulses and diverting our attention to what seems to be important in that particular moment, such as when the Scouse waitress returns to ask us whether we would like to see the dessert menu. In this instance, our attention is temporarily interrupted and we perceive all surrounding impulses at once: the music, our table partner, the waitress, the other people in the restaurant, their conversations, the general noise, the smell of food, the way the candlelight reflects on the cutlery, etc. We need a split second to re-adjust and focus our attention on the waitress and give her an answer, before we return to our conversation exactly where we left off. Similarly, we shift our attention when reading or studying with music in the background. Even though we are capable of dividing our attention between the study and the music, not everybody can study and listen to music simultaneously. It is very personal whether we can do this or not. Scientists believe that it is the amount of executive functioning we are able to assign to the task and for some, the music is simply too distractive. For those who can study with music in the background, it is important to divide the music into instrumental music and tunes with lyrics. There are people who can study with instrumental music, but everything crumbles with the advent of lyrics. This phenomenon can also be observed the other way around. More so, in those who can study with musical lyrics in the background, it also depends on the language. A person could be reading whilst a soprano sings a piece from Wagner's *Die Walküre*, but lose track altogether when they hear English singer-songwriter Adele lamenting. Hearing lyrics in a known or familiar language can be distracting at the same time as reading, as it mixes with what we read, while a foreign language can happily co-exist during our studies.

Another change of attention or shift in focus (yet another executive function) happens more subtly when the music in the background suddenly changes to a tune we recognise and which holds a particular memory, emotion or meaning for us. Our attention is shifted away from the conversation and to the music: we are actively listening to the music. The moment the music changes into a recognisable song, our frontal lobe shifts our attention away from the conversation towards the music. Emotions, memories and feelings are triggered and even expressed. We go so far as to change the topic and share the memories triggered by the song with our table partner and the waitress, who has returned with the dessert.

A similar shift in attention happens when we put on music at home—actively choosing the record and the artist and immersing ourselves in the music. All the brain areas are revisited as we lose track of time and space and listen with all our attention to the music, only to open our eyes and find ourselves sitting in the Royal Albert Hall with a thousand other people listening. The transition from pyjamas to tuxedo and vice versa has happened in the vast network of our mind, where we can either be at home being transported to a concert hall or sitting in the concert hall being transported to our living room. Active listening engages the whole brain and allows for memories and feelings to emerge, experiencing the music with our minds, as well as our bodies, feeling the space, the people or absence of them, and the music. Exposing ourselves to live performances, however, adds another layer to the experience of active listening. Our bodies perceive waves and frequencies in the space in which we are sitting, maybe even having physical contact with the person sitting or standing next to us, generating a collective experience which is shared through the presence of our bodies and minds. In other words, put on some ear protection and stand in front of the bass speaker during a live gig. You may not hear more than the bass of the music, but you will certainly feel the beat, which will add yet another layer to the experience we call music.

3
A NEW WAY OF LISTENING

With the advent of electronic and electrical instruments in the 1950s, music changed radically. Whether the screaming riffs of Jimi Hendrix burning his Fender Stratocaster, or Karl Heinz Stockhausen's synthesisers, technology has opened up a plethora of possibilities which has only accelerated with the advent of the computer and other technological devices incorporated into modern day music. Therefore, not only the music has changed but also the way we play and, more importantly, the way we listen has changed. Music, moving through the notion of organised sound, has become an overstimulating wall of bits and bytes, of bleeps and blips, all creating new sounds. Our brains have had to adapt to these new sounds, and fast, as the music itself has been changing. We have missed such radical jumps in recent years, as we seem to have reached the abattoir of hope when it comes to new music. Maybe artificial intelligence will help us out, or perhaps make things worse?

Anyhow, the way we perceived music up until the middle of the twentieth century was based on the sound of the instrument or the voice in its natural state. Through widely available recording technology at the beginning of the twentieth century, we were able to capture sound and replay it, marking a point in history that allowed for a recorded performance to be revisited again and again, to hear it in precisely the same way as it was initially performed. We transitioned from a single musical occurrence to music as an artefact, something physical, other than frequencies and waves. Prior to this, and this is still the case, performances varied ever so slightly, even though the musicians were highly trained and skilled.

Let me exemplify this through two of the most influential recordings in jazz, Miles Davis's *Kind of Blue* and *Bitches Brew*. These albums could not be more different, and yet they are connected through their musical heritage. There is more than ten years between their making. During those ten years, not only music went through a significant change, but more so the context and circumstances around it; it was a time of political and social uproar, when the fight for equal rights was initiated, challenging more than just social injustice, but the very right for existence.

Kind of Blue (1959) is mostly based around the 12-bar jazz blues scale. It follows traditional jazz music, up to that point in time, when musical phrases were based around known expressions like the work song. Even though *Kind of Blue* was the birth of the ballad, the structure of the songs on the album did not violate the expectations of the listeners, as they were accustomed to the 12-bar blues. We can predict the next step in the music (remember the 'Auld Lang Syne' experiment) and follow it, relishing the soothing sounds of the trumpet. Davis wanted to step away from the uncertain postwar years, shaped by the fast and furious bebop with greats like Charlie Parker and Dizzy Gillespie. The concept of *Kind of Blue*, however, was originally based on the African ballet, as attested by Miles Davis in his 1980s appearance on the Dick Cavett Show. He went on to describe the sound of the African thumb piano, which he wanted to emulate with his trumpet sound. However, things did not turn out the way he planned and *Kind of Blue* was the result.

Bitches Brew (1969), on the other hand, was a reflection of the turbulent years of the 1960s, based on no agreed structure or tonality, forcing the musicians to create something out of thin air and the listener to find a way of understanding the music. The album is embodied cognition as it reflects the world through the ears of the performer, translating it to the context of the listener, while changing what we are listening to and how we listen. The music is liberated from any convention of tonality or structure. New instruments, such as synthesisers and electric guitars, were mixed with effects on the trumpet and saxophone, creating a completely new soundscape. If you have never experienced *Bitches Brew*, I suggest you play it in its entire beauty.

What you will experience while listening to this album comes close to cognitive overload. You will be amazed by the scale and depth of the music. You are trying to understand the musical event, your brain is looking for hierarchies, and your cognitive economy grasps everything it possibly can, to make it through to the end. It is difficult to imagine that how we perceive something so out of our depth—everything we could possibly want is at our fingertips so the odds that we have never heard experimental contemporary music are rather small—can stun our brain into a default mode, looking for structure only to find none. Our neurons are all firing, our networks are moving between the known and the unknown, and synapses are slowly searching for new points they can attach to, in order to learn how to handle this new stimulus. The fact that they cannot control it activates pleasure centres in our brains, releasing different hormones like dopamine and oxytocin, elevating us into a natural high, creating pleasurable connections with what we are hearing—musical euphoria. Our experience with something completely new has enriched our musical vocabulary and opened new pathways of prototyping and exemplar cognitive approaches, categorising unfamiliar musical information towards a new way of listening.

4
THE IMPROVISING LISTENER

Improvising in such a context is like listening to something for the first time. We must find things we know before we can make sense of it, as otherwise our brain will remain in a constant state of limbo in-between order and disorder. During the recording of *Bitches Brew*, or even before, there were no agreements or notations to guide the musicians. They had to rely on their musical knowledge and *musical intuition*, if you wish. As a neuroscientist it is very difficult to admit to such concepts as intuition and instinct, as they cannot be measured directly or empirically. Nonetheless, they form an important part of our lives as we often follow our intuition rather than our rational minds, which allows for the most wonderful encounters. Walking into the recording session, therefore, must have felt like being a child again, with no rules or boundaries to influence our judgment about the world around us. Dislodging any sense of logic during the recording session permitted unfiltered and spontaneous thoughts to emerge and flow, something which has become part of the musical fingerprint of each musician and, in turn, listener. As improvising listeners, we follow the path of the musicians, without knowing it. We are lifted by the drums and bass and swirled around by the trumpet and keyboards, while trying to hold on to the saxophone melody; then all of a sudden we are dropped into a deep hole of silence, only to be propelled out of it to hang between melody and rhythm. We are constantly analysing the music, making decisions as to where it goes next, which turn it will take and where it will lead us. We struggle to anticipate the next move, yet follow the music in our own way, experiencing, listening, learning. In this context, saxophonist John Coltrane, during the recording sessions of *Ascensions* (1966), gave absolutely no guidelines to the musicians, except that they had to finish on a crescendo—the gradual increasing of sound to finish at the loudest point. He forced the musicians, and us as listeners, to explore our own musical limits. The opening movement, however, is based on a motif, introducing a starting point, a sort of seed, from which the avant-garde tree can grow from the roots of past musical experiences, our social context, and what we already know. The musicians take off from there, mixing their own experiences into the loose framework, challenging the listener and themselves to explore new ways of listening, investigating phrases, tones and harmonies, as well as tonal and atonal hierarchies. Each individual voice played could have been a new point of departure, changing the structure, and introducing a sheer infinite number of possibilities where the music could have gone next.

The way we listen is supplemented with new information, or even the lack thereof, such as in *Ascensions*, and everything we hear reaches our brains simultaneously. We struggle to filter or choose. Our dorsolateral prefrontal cortex shifts between enabling and disabling a decision, only to find itself stuck in the minute moment between those two states, allowing for new information to be incorporated into our memory. The more we listen, the more we lose our sense of panic and fear and start to find paths which were hidden to us before; we begin to get accustomed to a lack of structure. We immerse ourselves in this free-floating state, allowing our own interpretations to take over, integrating our emotions, behaviour and cognition into the way we hear the music. All of this happens simultaneously while we experience the album as listeners.

It is yet again an elegant balance between *ratio* and *emotio*, between the known and the unknown, and the ability of our brain to recruit multiple areas to build our library. We improvise through doing. We also improvise through perception, when we listen, see or experience something completely new. We need the pre-learned to satisfy our cognition, which helps us to make sense of the world, until the moment we encounter something we have never encountered before. It is then that we have to fall back on the neural trinity of emotion, behaviour and cognition to understand the unconventional and unique. It is the freedom to choose freedom.

5
FREEDOM TO
CHOOSE FREEDOM

The concept of free will has been argued and discussed by philosophers for more than two millennia. The question, however, still remains: what is free will and how does it actually work in our brain? Philosophers and scientists alike believe that free will is a decision-making process, which is free of any constraints. This sounds very much like our earlier definitions of improvisation and creativity. There are different views on what free will actually is. There is the religious concept, which takes into account an omnipresent divinity. Consequently, if we support this notion we make choices based on the knowledge that a 'higher being' is influencing them. Another view is grounded in ethical thought, which argues that individuals can be held morally responsible for their actions. Against this backdrop, science in general abnegates the notion of free will arguing that only the illusion of free will is created based on finite rules and parameters. This scientific view, consequently, tries to measure free will and create a framework in which it can exist. This also corresponds to the philosophical view; however, this does not use measuring tools to try and understand free will but maintains that an action can only have a certain outcome in relation to the given circumstances in that particular moment. This would mean that every act of free will is confined to a Zimmer frame, not being able to run freely but being constrained by its own capabilities. At this point philosophers split into two camps: the compatibilists and the incompatibilists. The former believe that free will does not exist and the latter that it must exist. The framework of how it exists and what this means for the way we, as humans, navigate the world, are concepts still being debated.

In the face of this, science, and especially the neuro-cognitive discipline, has set out to understand the notion of free will through experimentation. Researchers have shown that our brain has the ability to trigger a decision up to six seconds before we are actually aware of that decision. John-Dylan Haynes and his colleagues created an experiment in which human subjects had to execute a movement task. These motor tasks consisted of being directed to press a button with either their right or left hand, while lying in an fMRI scanner. While the participants were pressing the buttons the researchers scanned their brain activity. What they were trying to ascertain was whether or not free will is involved when making a decision to press either the right or left button—the freedom to make a choice. What they found was that areas in the prefrontal cortex, the hippocampus and the amygdala were activated when pressing either button. Besides showing the activation of these areas, what surprised the scientists was that there was a delay in brain activity between the decision making and the actual pressing of the button. The scans revealed that the brain made the decision to press either button before the subjects were aware of which button to press. This means that free will is something executed by our brain, rather than by an aware and conscious human being. But once again it is more complex than this and is not simply a split between body and mind. It is the speed of processing incoming stimuli, such as vision or sound, which pass through our different memories, cognitive functions and hierarchical organisations, minimising the perception error. Everything we see or hear is based on pre-learned and internalised information, and in order to understand the world with the speed that is necessary, we make predictions, actively imposing assumptions and beliefs onto the world, as the world, in turn, does onto us; this is the idea of embodied cognition as described above. The findings of Haynes and colleagues, therefore, do not reflect a division between body and mind, but are a reflection of the state of mind we have described above, the minute moment between activity and inactivity in the dorsolateral prefrontal cortex. This is the precise moment when unfiltered and spontaneous information can emerge, i.e., the moment of improvisation. The incoming information is perceived and processed, compared with stored information, a decision is made, and new information is updating what we already know. And all of this happens between the moment of seeing an arrow pointing left and pressing the left button. It might be presumptive to say that free will and our understanding of improvisation and creativity in brain functions, such as the DLPFC and their associated networks, are embodied cognition. More research will be needed to look into the relationship between what we see, what we do, and the how, why and what. But it certainly is food for thought.

With this in mind, we could say that experiencing music and thus linking the experience to our memories and emotions broadens the way we experience music in any given moment. It is the choice to choose freedom and expand our musical framework, either by ourselves when listening and playing, or by a trained music professional in education or music therapist in healthcare. Even though we will stay within our own musical framework, whether we are listeners, patients or students, the context in which it can take place is expandable, as well as any additional and well-balanced input towards a commonly achievable goal, like well-being.

Piet Mondriaan's (1872–1944) *Compositie met gele lijnen* (1933) illustrates the choice to choose freedom within a framework, hence, creating the illusion of freedom. When looking at this painting, the first thing we see is a plain white space framed by four yellow lines. In our example of musical experience and ability to improvise, the white space is personal experience accompanied by our musical baggage, which we have accumulated up until this point in time. The space is framed by four yellow lines, which indicate the framework of our experiences. Having a closer look at the yellow lines, however, we see that each of them has a different width. Now imagine that the yellow lines are not fixed to the canvas, but are stickers, which we can freely move around the canvas. The lines do not constrain the white space, but narrow or widen it, depending on how we move them. We have to see the painting as a dynamic object where we can add or deduct experiences at will, as our brains are dynamic organs, changing, adapting, learning and making decisions as to where to go next. We are not always able to expand those contexts ourselves or move the lines to widen our view. In these cases, we need to sit back and allow John Coltrane, Karl-Heinz Stockhausen or Tupac Shakur to move the lines for us.

6
THE ART OF IMPROVISATION

The art of improvising links the origins of what we understand and perceive as music with the way we understand our own creative abilities at large. To say that we are not able to improvise would take away one of the strongest cognitive abilities we possess. Moreover, we use improvisation in everyday life, whether it is at home, in education or in therapeutic music settings. Researching improvisation, and the way it is used in educational as well as clinical settings, opens up a Pandora's box of abilities that we, as humans, have either forgotten or have covered up with the blanket of social embarrassment imposed on us. We are made to believe that we cannot improvise anymore—musically or in everyday life—as it means losing structure, immersing ourselves in chaos and surrendering to what is believed as 'free will', which has *apparently* been eradicated by science. But improvisation is so much more than the notion of free will, structure or social acceptance of what we deem to be pleasant or unpleasant. In the Western jazz tradition, we see improvisation as a key aspect of being able to perform this style of music. Many will say it is a pleasant incorporation of the freedom a musician is at liberty to take in order to elevate a written piece of music. However, as soon as a *freer* version of jazz is played, say, for example, John Coltrane's *Ascensions* or Miles Davis's *Bitches Brew*, even though they are two key albums in the development and evolution of modern and popular music today, quite a few listeners would not make it beyond the A-side of these LPs. This is because the music, as already mentioned, does not necessarily follow a tonal, rhythmical or harmonious constellation, something very important to Western ears. Upscaling improvisation and placing it into a wider cultural context, this art form is known well beyond the Western jazz tradition. Hindustani music, Gregorian chant and even the *The Art of Fugue* by Johann Sebastian Bach know improvisation. Improvisation is more than a clinical or musical tool for experts. It is part of our diverse cultures. It is a musical subculture within the cultures in which we live. Improvisation allows us to communicate and share, it can start revolutions, knows fear and rebellion, and yet courage and honesty are its constant companions. Our humanly passion fuels improvisation and the creative, unstructured, and seemingly free process it entails, regardless of background, gender or ethnicity.

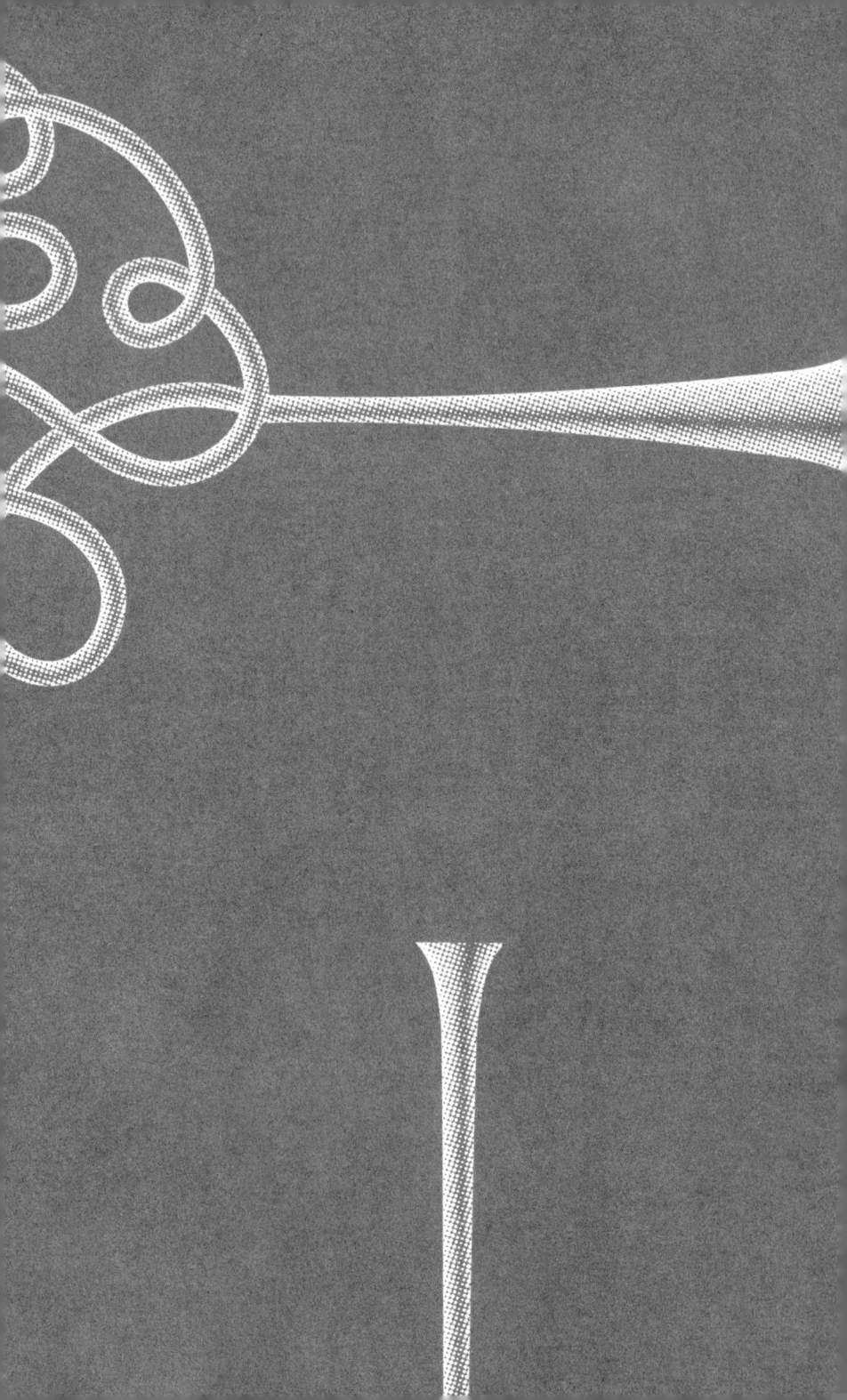

PART IV

IMPROVISE THIS!

1

HUMANe

In earlier chapters we have focused on the way we learn how to improvise, how the brain makes music, and what it means to experience the world through embodied cognition. More so, we have seen that our brains are wired in such a way that improvisation is innately built into our neural fingerprint, and therefore is not exclusive to a few, those blessed with creative talent. We can learn how to improvise, as we have merely forgotten that we are already improvising every day, using overlapping and similar brain networks whether we have a conversation or improvise musically. It is all about the content of our mental rucksack from which we are improvising that determines the outcome. To do so, we do not use our brains alone but also our bodies in the elegant dance of cognition, emotion and behaviour. After all, we are not just our brains, but a combination of mind and matter that allows us to be aware of the world around us. We think, therefore we are. We perceive, we process, and we make assumptions while we learn how to navigate the world. One of these important parts of learning and navigating is creativity and improvisation. To improvise is to learn. It means to open ourselves to new and unknown experiences, free of what we already know. Our brains need to be stimulated, otherwise they will fall into patterns which in the long run will not utilise the whole network the brain has to offer. Do not get me wrong, routine is a good thing and will get you through certain tasks, but try to break your routine every now and then to stimulate your brain: brush your teeth with your non-dominant hand, take a different route to work *without* the aid of satellite navigation, or ask some *very* good friends to drive you blindfolded a few miles outside of town, and leave you to find your way back home without the aid of your mobile phone or credit card. All of these stimulate your brain, push your body to a certain limit as you have to navigate and explore the world around you differently and in a novel way, and most of all such situations will trigger your ability to improvise. Dusting all the networks and synapses, removing the cobwebs from the gears, transistors and quanta will allow you to kick-start those connections. Yes, it is all about learning as much as possible. However, it is also about forgetting all of it when you have to improvise, which allows for the *creatio ex nihilo*, as John Coltrane has so famously put. Improvisation is more than recycling, reframing and reproducing. It is the act of making something new, something unprecedented. Cognitive psychologist Robert Weisberg has argued that to think creatively will always be based on *something*, even though we do not know what that *something* is. Even when we remove everything from a given space, there will still be molecules or quarks. If we remove these, there will still be waves. Even if we could reverse engineering to the Big Bang, it still may not be possible to recreate the point of absolute nothingness. But is this actually the point? If there would be nothing, not even quarks, waves and matter, then we would not be able to improvise at all. Moreover, we would not exist in such an environment, which would make improvisation and creativity non-existent. Therefore, it is not so much whether creating something out of nothing actually means nothing, but rather the ability to rearrange what we know on a molecular level, where unknown, unfiltered and unplanned combinations are possible in the wide ether of our biological minds. We cannot have an epiphany about something that we do not know or have no memory of. But we can create a new line of thought and the more alternative views and memories we have, the stronger will be the illusion of having created something out of absolutely nothing. It is the freedom to choose freedom that gives rise to the *creatio ex nihilo* moment and allows for innovation in-between the enabling and disabling of brain networks.

To illustrate this, let us take a look at one of the largest networks on earth: the internet. This is a massive non-biological global network, which gains constant and a seemingly infinite amount of information. While it is bound to the restrictions of hardware, not like our brains, which can process information on less power than a light bulb, it learns, links and processes information. Its capacity to grow reaches new daily heights, as we are feeding Google at any given moment throughout our day. It does so through sophisticated deep-learning algorithms, where prompts or questions we ask are linked to everything it can find out about it online. When we ask the machine to look up a certain word or phrase, it automatically saves the query, not only for our search history, but in its *own memory* so as not to be surprised by such a search query again. It remembers it, learns from it and applies it to other searches—an ever-growing network fed by our own curiosity. You can compare this to any flat-pack furniture. If you have never built a cupboard from a flat pack, you will follow each step in the manual to construct the cupboard. After having built a few of these, the contents of the box—a few loose parts, some screws and Allen keys—will no longer surprise you, and you will have prepared proper tools for the job before opening a new box: you have learned to use your own tools, rather than the ones shipped in the flat pack. The machine does the same thing—looking, linking, evaluating and learning. There is only one major difference; why do we as humans end up with spare screws we cannot account for in the instructions or the build itself? Maybe someone accidently packed one too many, or we have not followed the instructions properly. Well, time will tell whether the cupboard will stay standing! A machine algorithm does not forget a screw, as it follows instructions precisely. It will follow a pre-programmed flow chart, analysing the data, comparing it and looking for matches to build the cupboard correctly. When we search for the term 'deep learning' online, we will get around sixteen million hits, which all relate to the words deep learning. This is only the surface, as it has looked for matches of the words *deep* and *learning*. Even on page twenty-five, it links the two words and searches beyond the context of computer science and robotics and will relate deep learning to everything that can be associated with *deep* and *learning*.

Such learning algorithms have become more sophisticated over the years, such as the earlier mentioned ChatGPT, which is able to write song lyrics, or tries to fool you into thinking that you are talking to a human being rather than a machine. But as described already, as impressive as they are they still come with noteworthy flaws, like not having lived the lyrics they are writing, hence us not believing them. Nick Cave famously reacted to a ChatGPT lyric in the 'style of Nick Cave' for this very reason[26]—I will spare you the somewhat strong language Mr Cave used. Another serious flaw is the lack of being able to improvise.

2
DEEP LEARNING
AND THE BRAIN

If we compare the internet to our brains, we can see parallels in how we learn, process and consolidate knowledge, even though a machine, or the internet, *thinks* differently. Can a machine improvise like humans? No, it cannot, as they are two different things. Can a machine improvise at all? Well, not quite yet. Looking at the similarities, the brain was born from a single egg and sperm, which initiated the division of cells. Deep learning is similar to this only in that it does not use sperm and egg cells but an algorithm, a command or prompt, which has been programmed into a computer network. Like a cell in our bodies and in our brain network, the algorithm cannot *survive* on its own. It needs input and information based on other algorithms. Different prompts will trigger different networks, which in turn convey specific information. As soon as the deep learning algorithm has gathered enough information and partnered with other algorithms, it can start to link, evaluate and learn, making simple choices and communicating information. These connections are not yet consolidated as they are based on exploration rather than repeated prompts. Our brain, as we have seen, learns in a similar way, consolidating pathways that have been laid down exploratively through neural plasticity and the way neurons and synapses wire together. If the connections are not used, our brain simply gets rid of them; hence the famous phrase, use it or lose it. A computer algorithm will not necessarily *lose* the connection, it will more so remember and save the way it has come to that solution.

Visualisation of how we and machines learn: it starts with one information block.

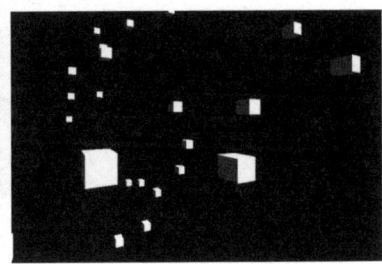

Associations are made with other information blocks.

This in turn can be compared to human cognitive economy, which involves not having to use all the brain's power to identify a problem as it has already been solved. While more information is entered into the system, the algorithm starts to cluster it into groups, which again will be connected, creating a network within a network. As soon as the clusters are consolidated, the algorithm does not have to compare a new prompt with everything already there, but only with the clusters, before analysing and linking the prompt with information in one cluster alone. If input matches information from two clusters, those two clusters are linked. The more information, the more complex the network and the more different clusters are interlinked as the information is overlapping. These connections allow for information to be retrieved faster and more efficiently. In a way it resembles how the brain is growing its network but, here again, do not be fooled by this comparison, as the deep learning algorithm and the brain are two different things.

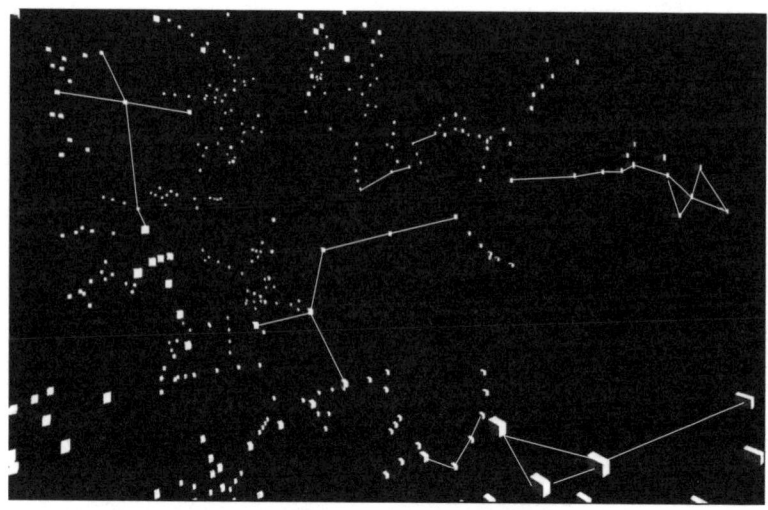
Associations/information blocks are being connected.

The moment you type a random word into a search engine, it will compare millions of pages containing that word. To do that quickly it compares groups, clusters and, in the last stage, the information within a cluster group. The search engine translates our question to the internet through this series of algorithms and prompts. Once the prompt has been answered, the network clears the pathways and saves the most economic route to find that information, should you look for it again in the future. It does so by saving all sorts of data on your computer, in your browser, and through your IP address. All of these we accept when we agree to cookies, essential or not. The algorithm therefore increases its ability to access information faster, consolidating pathways that are used more often, thus reducing the processing power to a minimum. To bring it back to the biological, imagine your first kiss. The moment you read this, your mind unleashes an avalanche of thoughts, feelings and maybe even behaviours. You think back to the surroundings, your age, the day, the person, the music, the sweaty palms and the feeling. It is not about the quality of the kiss; it is the actual experience of the kiss. It is all associated with that one phrase: your first kiss. Now type 'your first kiss' into a search engine. Disappointing, isn't it?

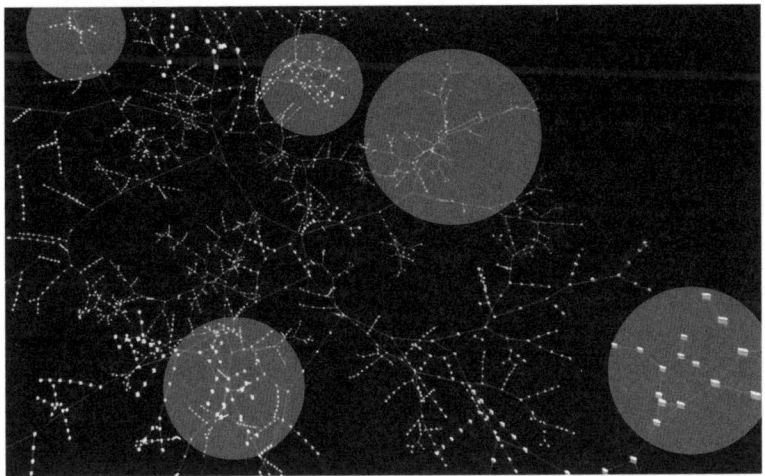

Association clusters are being formed.

The brain as well as the algorithm are constantly associating, searching for and linking clusters of information in order to preserve energy. However, there is a significant difference: deep learning is confined to the physical boundaries of hardware. If we do not build more data centres, more microchips and fibreglass cables, there will be a limit to the information that can be stored. We, on the other hand, do not store information, we story it, with our senses, cognition, emotions and behaviour. The machine has to rely on statistical significance, i.e., which paths have been used more often, what makes more sense as it follows and flows from logical steps, which paths can be traced. In such cases, a term prompted into a search engine will always bring up information directly related to the term, either mentioning the term or being associated with the term stemming from logic. Against this backdrop, does the statistically significant fade with every page at the bottom of the search engine that you follow up? At page 367, the relationship between certain terms will be so alienated that it will be difficult to find a resemblance between the two words we have typed into the search engine. The deep learning algorithm uses the smallest similarities based on logic associated with the prompt.

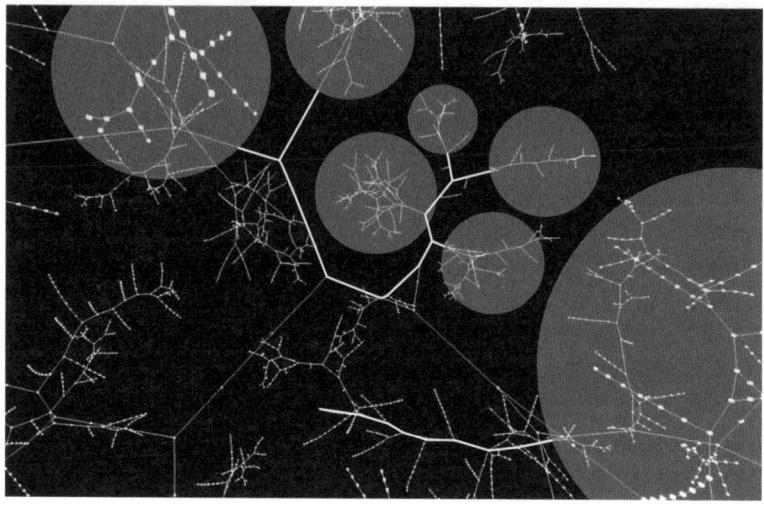

Association clusters are consolidated and connections strengthened.

Clusters can no longer be matched, information no longer compared, and *spontaneity* is not something that can be built on logic and statistics. Creativity and improvisation is exactly that moment of spontaneous, albeit conscious, choice to link two absolutely unrelated and crazy ideas, which can only emerge when we let go of conscious choice, and embrace the freedom to choose freedom, with unconscious, unrelated, unfiltered and outright ludicrous ideas emerging. Take a *Blueberry Muffin* and a *Rolls Royce Jet Engine*. They have absolutely nothing in common and will not pop up in a search engine unless somebody somewhere has had a blueberry muffin next to a RR jet engine or has tried to bake one with the other. Statistically, however, this is next to zero. This spontaneous *jump* between clusters, this exchange of cockeyed and unrelated harebrained ideas is so far only possible in the human mind where neurons and synapses find themselves in a temporary lapse of reason and allow for creativity, for improvisation to emerge.

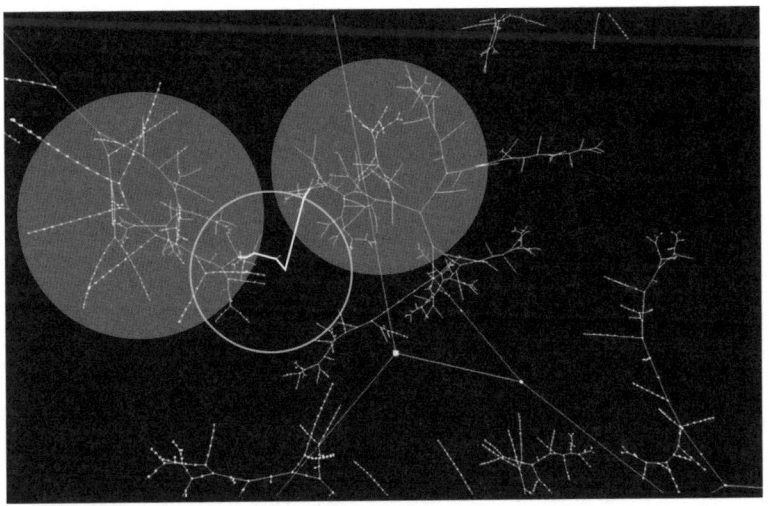

Spontaneous 'jump' between two unrelated clusters;
the *creatio ex nihilo* in action.

3

MACHINES DO
EXPERIENCE MUSIC
BUT WE JUST DO NOT KNOW
HOW TO MEASURE IT

Machines and algorithms may never be able to improvise and make the jump beyond the logical and statistical. In the end, we are trying to imitate humans, rather than looking for the actual talents of the machines in conversation. However, we can use algorithms and machines to increase our abilities, whether it is their computing power or their ability to enhance the way we think. If anything, machines should make us question our choices and the way we look at the world. At some stage we may become mere digital immigrants, entering a world which has moved beyond the humanly understandable, trying to ask the right questions to expose the workings of artificial intelligence and machine-learning algorithms. In these instances, our ability to improvise, to be creative, will allow us to look beyond the machine and the abilities we have programmed into it. The way we learn is literally in our pockets. Fifteen to twenty years ago we dismissed this as science fiction but look where we are today. In another twenty years we may have cracked the way we improvise, what consciousness entails, and how we experience the world. Even though we cannot predict the future, we have to ask ourselves how to learn, what to learn and why to learn about the world if we want to be able to understand the cognitive and ethical uncertainties of the digital age. We have to stay focused on what we want to get out of the silicon age. It will be about challenging academic traditions and the impact our behaviours have on society, as well as the way in which we define and allow human-centred AI into our lives. Against this backdrop, it is our values, traditions and heritage that make us human. It is the way we learn to improvise, to interact and to be creative in a world that is changing beyond recognition. It is our innate curiosity and willingness to change the world, to question paradigms and to move beyond what we have learnt. We may feel vulnerable, maybe even overwhelmed and insecure, when considering technological developments. But it is the combination of artificial intelligence and human intelligence which we can benefit from (part 5 will show one example of this interaction). Understanding the way we improvise does not only teach us about how our brains work, but it also allows us to find the boundaries of what we as humans are capable of and, in turn, the limitations of the technologies with which we surround ourselves. Where human and machine meet, without hierarchies and imposed superiority, lie the possibilities for a symbiotic co-existence of algorithms and brain networks. So far, we cannot say how an equal conversation between artificial and human intelligence will look, without the one being the coder of the other. Even though AI algorithms are already writing music—give an AI the prompt to write a Beatles song and it will create one which sounds exactly like the original band—there is something in the music that is linear, predictable and, to some ears, flat. It goes without saying that AI has seeped into our daily musical experience, with most advertisement and video game music already being composed by AIs. But to go so far as to say that AI will determine the next step in the evolution of music might be a bridge too far. We hear many voices claiming that AI will champion the next musical revolution, as Miles Davis, John Coltrane, Goldie or Iron Maiden have done. But it is about much more than spearheading. It is about the mirror which we as humans must constantly put in front of ourselves, reflecting on our own abilities, the abilities we want to pass on, and the boundaries which come with these. Only once we know our boundaries can we use our creativity to go beyond those borders, using artificial intelligence as an addition to our abilities. This is more in line with *augmented intelligence* rather than artificial intelligence, in its capacity to accompany and elevate our minds and mental abilities.

4
MUSIC AND THE METAVERSE

Today, at the heyday of the silicon age, we are used to music as a luxury consumer product, often not even noticing it anymore. When did you last pay attention to the background soundtrack in a movie or video game? Yet we wish to experience music as it is part of our emotional and conscious experience of the world.

During 2020–21, the pandemic accelerated the trend for digitisation. The importance of digital development towards new technological avenues increased as we were forced to work from home. The technology to do so, however, did not meet the requirements needed to give a comparable experience of face-to-face human interaction. It is one thing to have a conversation in a pub or while walking the dog, and quite another to talk to a screen. What happens between the two screens is unknown. Where does the data go, who is listening in, what about our privacy?

While technological efficiency has been slowly improving, digital human interaction has not been addressed in a satisfactory way. It does not really matter how many online calls we have, it will never replace the real thing as we cannot *savour* the other person and their subtle movements, e.g., a twitching leg when nervous, their body language and *their* projection of embodied cognition in the world. During the pandemic, we all had encounters where we met people for the first time in the online environment, and once we met them face to face, the person's appearance was completely different to what we experienced on screen. The assumptions that our mind has made about that person's bodily features have been seldom met, as a two-dimensional screen representation simply does not match a three-dimensional representation in time and space.

Many believe that the metaverse—a virtual space where we will interact with each other and the environment with the help of virtual reality (VR), augmented reality (AR) and extended reality (XR) technologies—is the next logical step in online meetings and social interaction.

Can music be integrated within the broader narrative of the metaverse and help musicians of any level create new experiences for their audience?

A great part of enjoying music is forming connections with your favorite artists and other fans: millions have been hungry for live music during the last two years of the pandemic. We all want to belong and share experiences. This is the reason why we collect merchandise, go to concerts or festivals, hunt for autographs, and join meet-and-greet events. Metaverse is all about the community, as well [...].

The first cases from the metaverse are jaw-dropping. Amelia Kallman shares amazing stats: 'watching Travis Scott live in Fortnite..., was not one big group of 12.3 million people, but instead, the concerts were made up of 50 people each.' Thus, 'essentially, there wasn't one concert, but 250,000 co-occurring.' This fosters much more engagement than lockdown-induced YouTube videos of a show performed in an empty venue, right?

And talking about merchandise, what concert-goer doesn't love those amazing merch cannons? Lil Nas X has pioneered the way with his Roblox concert, distributing the 'merchandise that far outpaced their initial expectations, citing an eight-figure rate,' as *The Guardian* reports. 'Limits are non-existent in the metaverse,' claims Jon Vlassopulos, global head of music of video game developer Roblox.

(Emil Angervall, 2022: https://cryptoslate.com/music-to-grow-body-in-metaverse-start-new-age-of-connection-and-immersion/)

There are already many opportunities that a metaverse can offer when it comes to immersion and connection. But we also have to admit that we are still far away from a unified space where we can all interact in the way that we interact with each other in everyday life. Hardware, software, and our understanding of what it means to be part of a metaverse still have to be understood from an ethical as well as social impact point of view, before we can actually take the step into these environments. We have made the mistake before, by blindly accepting social media without taking bias, discrimination, hatred and exclusion into account. Today we look back and see what we should have done before allowing social media into our lives. We can only hope that we have learnt from this mistake in the past and approach the metaverse with an open mind and a careful and critical, as well as ethical, consideration before bringing it into the mainstream. This careful approach, however, seems to be wishful thinking, as social media knows how to manipulate us into something that we want, but don't necessarily need. This is not new to mass psychology and was already being researched in the 1920s, finding its peak in 1947 with "The Engineering of Consent", an essay by Edward Bernays. He argued that by translating social, scientific and professional approaches to the common customer through third parties who operate independently from the professionals, a need will be created in the customer, which is accelerated through the masses. This means that once we find third parties to promote something, the masses will adopt it. Moreover, it will create a fear atmosphere of missing out, with the latest influencers talking about the metaverse and how important it is for us; in the process they have not mentioned that self-centred greed and advertisement pay schemes lie at the core of their endorsements.

Accepting the metaverse completely, however, will require more than just mass psychology and propaganda. It will require hardware and computer power to connect parts of the metaverse, building an infrastructure which can be accessible to a wide range of people, to create a cohesive experience for everybody who has access to the internet. Once again, we see the bias in this endeavour, as the metaverse, as well as any other social media, only generates bigger exclusion and discrimination in the world as it is only accessible to communities with an internet connection. A similar bias is created when programming AI and the metaverse. As top-notch companies and universities usually reside in the Western world, or at least are tinted with the Western heritage, its employers and scholars programme their own Western biases into the algorithm or the digital environment. Only recently, we have become more aware of the diversity and inclusion which is necessary to be programmed into any digital environment. This is something which still needs much more work and will never include groups without, or with limited, internet access. However, as Emil Angervall says: "we should not lose track of the innovation and upheaval that the metaverse brings to music and will [bring] to the creative process of improvisation" (2022).

With this in mind, we should be aware that our ability to improvise will not be smothered by yet another digital gadget.

5
NON-FUNGIBLE TOKENS:
EMPOWERING MUSIC

Since 2021, decentralised technologies have been seeping into music. Non-fungible tokens (NFT), for one, are increasingly seen as a novel way of distributing audio and video content. At the same time, blockchain technology opens new potential for protecting and exchanging digital property rights. These technologies, however, do not come without their critics who claim that blockchain technology and NFTs are just inventions of Silicon Valley, who has run out of ideas and ways of making money—a kind of reversed Robin Hood effect, when the rich are taking even more from the poor to give back to the rich. Despite some level of truth in these claims, there is another side to blockchain technology, NFTs and decentralisation. They offer novel possibilities to create and develop inclusive exchanges, which are not biased or informed by economy-driven ideals of success, wealth and well-being. This is an idea of society where equality, diversity and democracy are values to strive towards, empowering the individual, as well as the group, to investigate what is good for the personal and the collective well-being. Here again, we have to mention that access to the internet is essential, and thus there will always be a shadow of exclusivity, even for those technologies advocating inclusion.

For artists, especially emerging talents, NFTs represent a viable new way of raising funds. Modern NFT platforms specialising in different aspects of music production, from funding to distribution, help them reach their audience, raise funds for their next tracks, and put the music out there for their fans to enjoy. Fans, in their turn, get a chance to support their favourite artists and experience material and emotive rewards. The latter is most in tune with the very spirit of music fanship: NFTs find a cosy nook in our mental libraries of emotions, memories and affiliations. Eric Elliot with Greenruhm.com says in his article: "[...] we're not buying JPGs. We're buying membership, identity, status, and a sense of ownership. And it is addictive."[27]

According to metaverse advocates, the new virtual worlds are bound to create an even more immersive—and addictive—experience.

Will this be the end of the human composer, the improviser, and our willingness to be creative? Why should we rely on our innate abilities, such as improvisation, if an external agent can do it for us? Maybe the preamble was right and we are allowing ourselves to be taken over by technology and thus lose our innate abilities, abilities we have relied on for millennia.

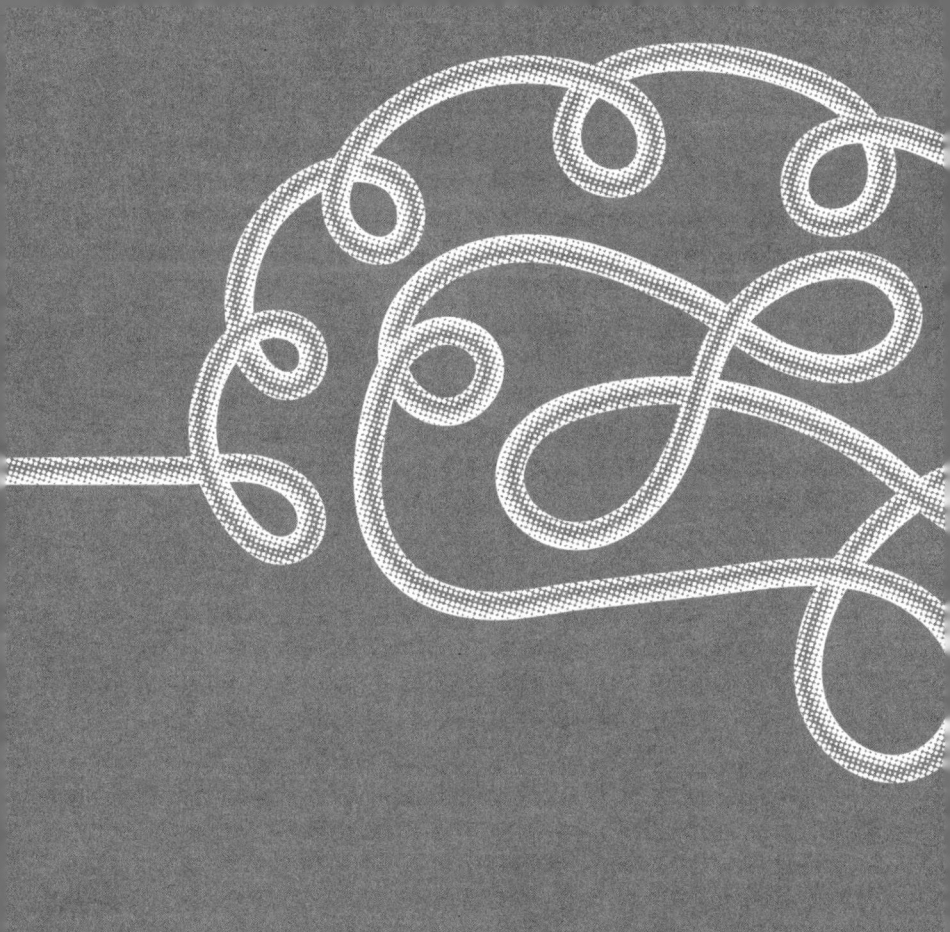

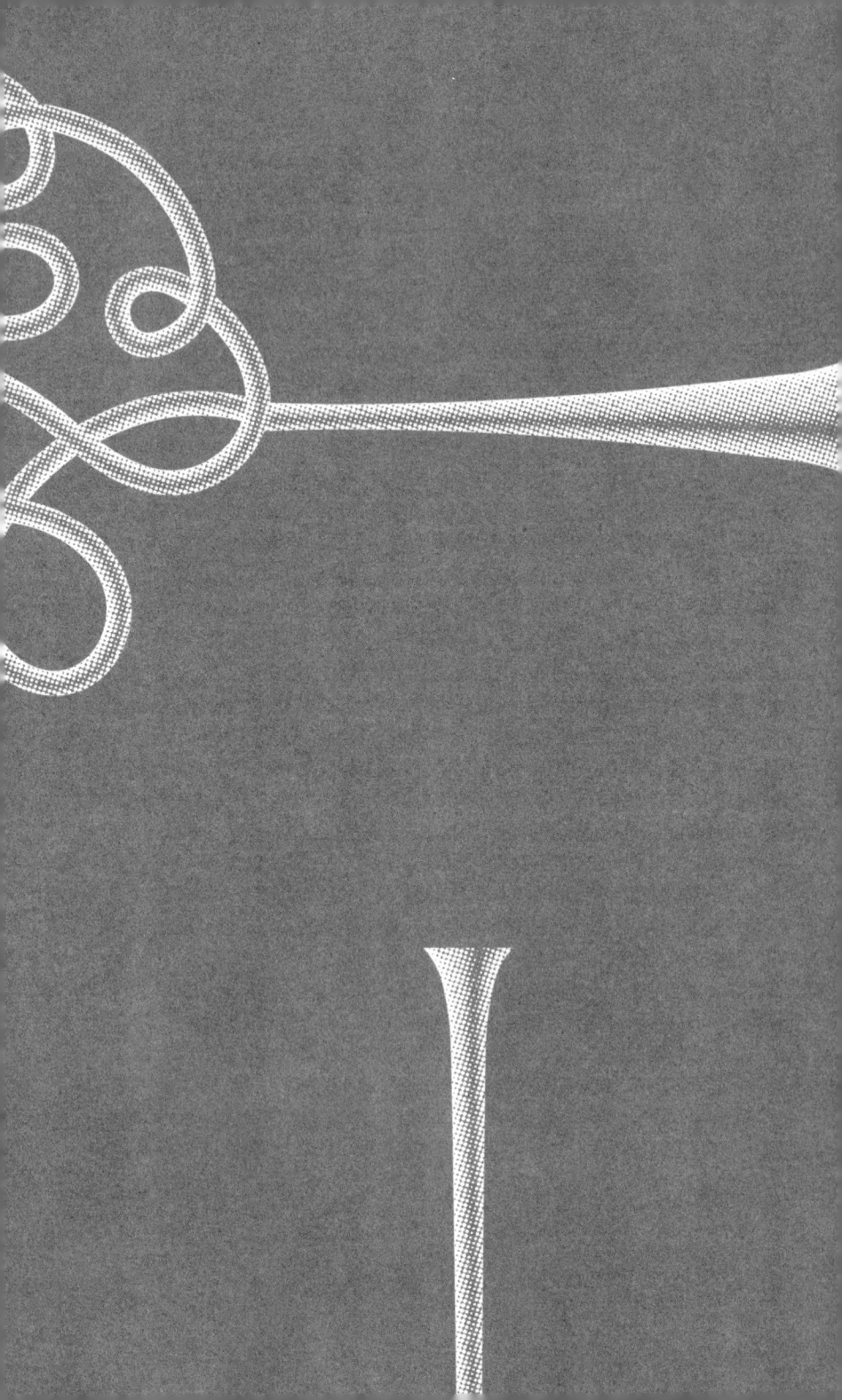

PART V

BEYOND MUSIC, IMPROVISATION AND THE BRAIN

1

MUSIC-BASED THERAPIES
AND INTERVENTIONS

Moving away from the somewhat bleak prospect of handing over our ability to improvise to technology, if we are not careful, let us revive the *human* agent in us and move into an area where machines cannot completely take over from humans: healthcare and therapeutic interventions.

As we have seen, musical interaction involves non-verbal communication. We are all musical beings with vast brain networks making music from waves and frequencies and linking emotions and behaviours to it. Furthermore, music is fundamentally interactive, creative, emotional and social. Generally, our appreciation for music builds on humanistic and psychological foundations, stressing the role of music as an inherently socio-emotional phenomenon. From this perspective, music-based therapies and interventions, or the clinical application of music, allows for (non-verbal) interaction and communication across different populations, ranging from premature babies and people with mental health issues, to end of life care in the elderly. Here, music is assumed to enable human expression of emotions, triggering cognitive networks, which are the exact building blocks of social connections, and can potentially facilitate and influence behaviours. Indeed, the socio-emotional aspects of music have been key to the recognition of music therapy as a profession within healthcare and well-being. Since the 1990s, neuroscientific research has helped to unravel, step by step, the mechanisms that drive socio-emotional and musical effects, and its influence on cognition and brain development, as well as our fundamental understanding of music. Such research has helped to explain how humans react to music emotionally, physiologically and behaviourally; why humans interact more easily with others when making music; and how this is affected as well as informed by our cognition.

However, it is one thing to improve our understanding of musical influences on the human body and brain. It is quite another to apply insights from music-based neurological research to the application and effects of *therapeutic* music-based interventions. Such an application is far from straightforward. The reason is that music therapists, when using music therapeutically, intervene at the individual level of a client's demand. Such individual client levels are often very specific and idiosyncratic, whereas current neurological insights can only approach a problem from a more general perspective, with the potential to investigate more in-depth functions and connectivity of neuropathology. The tension between the broad insights from neuroscientific research and the specificity of interventions in therapeutic settings makes it a matter of urgency to reconsider the working mechanisms of music-based therapies and interventions.

Awareness of musical parameters and their effect on cognition, emotion and behaviour is essential for the music therapy profession. Music is at the core of music therapy treatment; the therapeutic alliance is its vehicle. In music-based therapies and interventions the music is shaped to help a client develop in a specific direction. Such interventions serve merely as a cue for action, as music therapists do not search for a *thrill sensation* but attempt to provide musical triggers to enact change. This implies a thorough knowledge of the characteristics of music, potential cognitive and behavioural influences from a neuroscientific and neuropsychological point of view, and implementation of modern (music) technologies as a vehicle of interaction and measure. Furthermore, the ability to improvise in the moment, as each client is unpredictable in their reactions, is essential. This ability to improvise with somebody, rather than for the art itself, elevates improvisation to another level. It is not just learning and internalising music, but linking it to the behaviour and emotions of another human being and improvising around our assumption of the other person's world of perception. We have to understand how a combination of sounds and silences influences specific mechanisms in a human being, how pulse, volume, rhythm, melody, harmony and timbre affect the music-triggered mechanisms of an individual on several levels, from individualised therapeutic change to fundamental neuroscientific development. This gap can be bridged through our innate ability to improvise, triggering empathy as an associated executive function and our capacity to observe and *read* another human being. In an emerging digital society, this allows music therapists to practice within the wider context of a client's well-being, enabling therapeutic interventions fit for the twenty-first century.

2

DIGITAL SOCIETY

In Europe alone, the way we learn, play and interact has changed more in the past twenty years than in the previous 580, since the appearance of Gutenberg's printing press. With the average person now spending about eight hours a day interacting with one and sometimes two devices simultaneously, the amount of time it takes for a new technology to be used by fifty million people is unprecedented. According to Jay Gied, with "radio it took 38 years; for the telephone, 20; for television, 13; the world wide web, 4; Facebook, 3.6 years; for Twitter, 3; for iPads, 2 and for Google+, 88 days" (Gied, 2012:34).

With such fast societal changes, our brains also have to adapt to accommodate this transformation. Areas devoted to vision, or our working memory, have been substantially altered, with working memory decreasing and the representation areas for our thumbs increasing. We are evolving in light of the silicon age, adapting to the digitalisation of the world. However, as we have seen throughout this book, there are human faculties which are unique to humans. Nonetheless, with the advent of technological applications and the ever-growing amount of software, hardware, wearables and support gadgets, it seems that we have forgotten what we are looking for, what we want to measure and, more interestingly, whether we have developed these gadgets to find out more about the machine or about the human.

We fetishise technology to such an extent that we miss the actual purpose of a technological application—to support and enhance our lives and well-being—which consequently leads to the use of humans as proof of concept for the well-being of the machine, rather than the other way around. The interesting, and maybe controversial, question here is whether this is necessarily a bad thing or simply the next dip humanity has to go through before emerging with new knowledge to become better at being human.

Social interaction, cognition and behaviour are fundamental components of human life, widely studied in various scientific disciplines, and of growing importance in information and communication technologies (ICT). Current artificial intelligence technologies can exploit the large amounts of interaction data, allowing for exact measurements of interpersonal exchanges, communications and interactions.

The goal of music-based therapies fit for the twenty-first century is to develop new prototypes and new ways of understating our abilities, such as creativity and improvisation, through AI-based computational models and extended reality. Applying our improvisational skills to everyday life means that we have the responsibility to upscale those abilities by using therapeutic and pedagogical music interventions as a testbed. It is the study of the processes, and the design of novel AI-informed computational systems to enhance such interaction processes, that make music interactions a unique phenomenon.

How can we combine the human and the technological to build prototypes beyond smart devices? How can we build something that will make the difference between life and death, utilising the full potential of our creativity and amalgamating deep learning with our brain networks?

3

MUSIC, TECHNOLOGICAL DEVELOPMENT AND CLINICAL APPLICATION

There is little doubt that as we learn more about technology and how it affects us, we will be able to translate this into clinical applications across the life span. Research into music-based interventions in the twenty-first century involves cybernetics, artificial intelligence, linguistics, system theory, self-organisation, morphogenesis and algorithms. In this context, we have to keep asking the question whether we still measure what we intended to measure when it comes to perception, processing and execution in a socio-cultural context amidst technological advances. This forces us to re-examine this whole area as we are applying new modes of communication, interaction and well-being to fragile populations. We cannot simply go ahead and play some music to a baby in an incubator simply because a machine algorithm has calculated and advised us to do so, as this would overstimulate the baby's brain and possibly have a negative effect on recovery and brain development. Instead, we have to approach the baby with one tone, or the soft humming of a lullaby by the mother. It is a delicate balance between stimulation and calming, something so far only humans can do.

Within the music therapy profession, we encounter an increasing number of clients who grew up with technological developments as well as musical styles, like pop, hip-hop and dance music, associated with our digitalised society. Against this backdrop, the working field of the music therapist is in flux. Never before have clinical developments, methods and knowledge been so influential to the evolution of the music therapist. They must be flexible, mobile and innovative in their use of instruments, applications and/or digital devices. Some clients in either revalidation or medical settings are not able to use conventional instruments and technological developments in music offer alternatives catering to the abilities of different client populations.

In light of this, digitalisation has accelerated the development and evolution of technological advances in music therapy, allowing *easy-to-use* devices and interfaces to support the work of music therapists. Combining this with the ability to use improvisation as a clinical tool, music therapists are able to empower clients and allow them to participate again in life. We do not have to understand how a computer works, or the internet itself, to be able to use it and it is the same for different music technological advances. Therefore, it is important to move away from the technology itself and simply place it within the correct clinical context. Once we have familiarised ourselves with the possibilities out there we can then apply them in the most suitable way, to achieve the best possible therapeutic result for the client. *Moving away* from the technology, therefore, means to translate the native language of the device into a language understandable by the client and ultimately lead to the adaptation of the device or software towards the client's needs, something which cannot be entrusted to statistics and machine-learning algorithms alone.

4

IMPROVISATION AT THE HEART OF MUSIC-BASED THERAPIES AND INTERVENTIONS

Bringing together the different ways in which the brain understands, processes and represents music, have we reached the *harmonious union of all sciences*, as Kuhn has stated in his work *The Structure of Scientific Revolutions* (1962: 10), and the answer to the secret of improvisation? We are spoiled for choice when looking for this harmonious union, as we all come from different backgrounds and have had different experiences, and everyone will defend their own understanding from their own perspective. Can we understand music simply as a result of the vast network of neurons and synapses in our brains, all firing away at different rates, or does our subconscious actually choose between the brain and the body when experiencing a new multisensory stimulus, such as music? The different uses of music and improvisation in more applied settings, like music education, music therapy or music for health, offer a unique insight into what music can do for us, our children, and especially individuals struggling with physical or mental issues. The areas of healthcare, science and gaming are contributing to identify future directions for music, as well as music therapy interventions. Researching all available music technologies and identifying how and whether they can be used in music-based therapeutic settings will increase client well-being and health. Used in concert with hospitals, governments, institutions and business, we can deliver new knowledge, tools and solutions to meet the twenty-first century's most pressing challenges through music-based interventions.

Improving our understanding of music-based therapies in a digital society and inviting unlikely allies to the table can have far-reaching and unpredictable implications. Indeed, some of the world's greatest ideas have been total happenstance, never dreamed of by their creators. Innovation, however, does not stop at the highest point of excellence, but is only the beginning. In sum, it is necessary to include innovative technologies not only to research the relationship between auditory perception and hearing, but more so to inform clinical practice. With careful, active imaginative listening, we can learn to fine-tune our perception, processing and improvisation skills. This may, if we are alert, offer new insights into the effectiveness and importance of the trained use of music in clinical settings and beyond, feeding our *creatio ex nihilo*. Introducing technological advances into the clinic, however, has to be done carefully. As described above, there are still unresolved questions regarding technologies in, for example, the metaverse or any other augmented or virtual reality. However, we need to embrace these technologies in order to push forwards the frontiers of care and the application of music in different clinical populations. Technology is not meant to replace the caregiver, nurse or doctor, but to support them in their daily tasks, especially in one of the most vulnerable sections of society—(extremely) premature babies—as healthy aging begins at the moment of conception.

5

A GLIMPSE INTO THE FUTURE

Worldwide, preterm birth is the main cause of death for children under the age of five and was responsible for approximately one million deaths in 2022 (WHO). Extremely premature infants have a low survival rate as their bodies, brains and organs are not yet fully developed. These babies are between 24 and 28 weeks at birth and often weigh no more than 1,000 g. They are treated in neonatal intensive care units (NICUs), where incubators support their underdeveloped organs as much as possible. However, despite this highly specialised care, approximately 40% of infants born at 24–25 weeks will not survive. Of all babies who do survive, about another 60% will suffer life-long health complications (WHO). Every extra day an infant can spend in the safe environment of a NICU directly increases its chances of survival and quality of life.

At around 16 weeks, while still inside the mother's womb, the child can hear sounds, however, it cannot yet interpret these as sounds. From approximately 26 weeks' gestation, preterm infants will have the capacity to react to auditory stimuli. Within the womb, a foetus hears their mother's heartbeat, breathing and gait and shows recognition to the mother's voice and, in some circumstances, the father's voice as well. From 30 weeks onwards, the infant is able to distinguish between varying speech tones and timbres and is also able to process complex auditory sounds. This point likely marks the start of speech and language development. This shows us that the sonological or auditory environment in the womb is as important as its warmth, safety and nutrition.

When a child is born preterm, and is placed into an incubator, the incubator keeps the child alive as it creates a warm and secure environment where medical procedures can be administered. The noises inside and outside the incubator, however, do not resemble the sounds of the womb. In recent research our group has shown that music in the form of individual notes or sounds, provided by a specially trained music therapist, has beneficial effects on brain development, stress levels and overall health of a child born preterm. It stimulates the growth of the brain network and, furthermore, adds to the bonding process between parents and child, where parents feel connected with the infant through music. The therapist can incorporate any unwanted sounds, like the *beeps*, *peeps* and *hissing* of the air supply and heating apparatus, into individually chosen notes. Without such a therapeutic approach, the noise within the incubator could be harmful to the child. Some parents have reported that once at home their child could not fall asleep unless the hoover or hair-dryer was running; the sonic environment of the incubator has been imprinted onto the child's memory.

To avoid this, active noise cancelling (ANC) technology can be used. This is very similar to state of the art headphones. It is a sound system based on a high performing algorithm that actively reduces noise inside the incubator, creating a quieter and more comfortable environment. It works continuously over a broad range of frequencies adapting to various predictable and unpredictable sounds.

Unwanted vibrations, which turn into unwanted noise, are recorded and counteracted within milliseconds by an advanced AI algorithm. The vibrations and unwanted noise one would hear in the incubator are met with an opposing sound wave transmitted through the speakers. Microphones inside and outside the incubator record the sounds and contribute to enhancing the counter signal, thus creating a precise noise cancelling signal enabling a much quieter environment. Through directed speakers inside the incubator, the infant can be positioned in a sound-controlled circle; this is not a physical space but is created through the sound waves played from a transducer above the infant. This can be compared to standing in a shower cubicle, where the projected stream of water only hits a particular radius, allowing a person to be either wet or dry, depending on where they stand in the cubicle.

The ANC *Incubator* is a music-based therapeutic intervention incubator. It is a breakthrough in therapy for preterm infants and a wonderful example of augmented intelligence, where human intelligence and machine learning come together to work side by side. It is a controlled music therapy environment that monitors the child as well as creating a quiet environment, away from disturbing sounds both inside and outside the incubator and, at the same time, allowing positive sounds, like voices and music, to be introduced to the infant. Hearing speech is important for the child to develop their own language abilities. Administering NICU music-based therapies and interventions allow for brain development, as well as

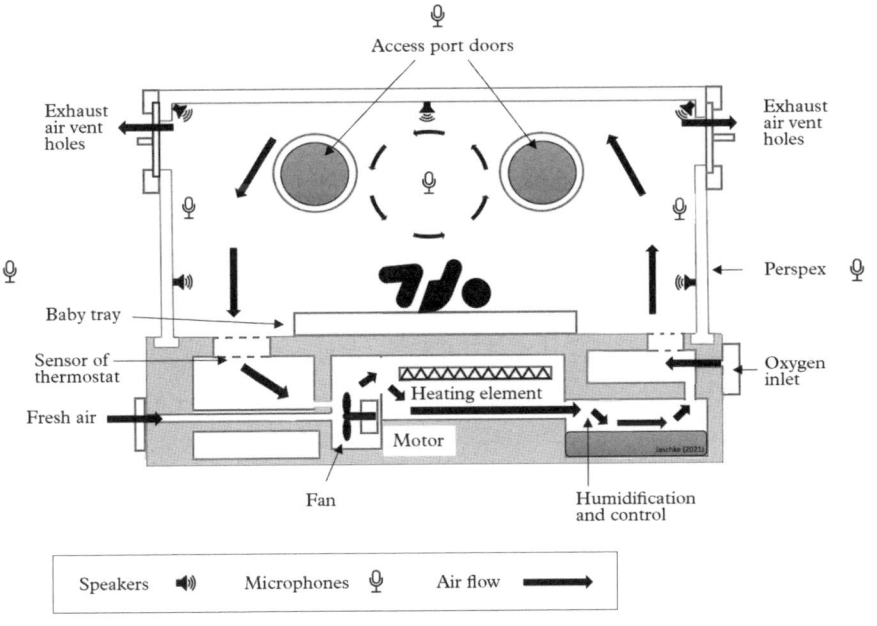

Access port doors

Exhaust air vent holes

Exhaust air vent holes

Perspex

Baby tray

Sensor of thermostat

Oxygen inlet

Fresh air

Heating element

Motor

Fan

Humidification and control

Speakers	Microphones	Air flow

(Jaschke & Bos, 2023)

minimising unwanted and potentially harmful noises, which add to the well-being and recovery of the neonate.

This is the point where both interventions and natural sonological surroundings come together, within a clinically implemented artificial framework, to reproduce the environment of each individual womb with controlled external inputs, such as the recorded womb sounds of the mother, the parents' voices, and music-based therapeutic interventions. Machine-learning algorithms, together with motion capture video recording, will help monitor the baby and support clinical care.

Imagine the ANC Incubator as a small-scale, physical metaverse, where the musical intervention is based around the experience of the child in the incubator, rather than the incubator simply being a space to keep the child alive. Transferring the immersive experience of the womb to the incubator could potentially have significant health recovery benefits. In turn, it would close the gap between cognition and movement and how these relate to each other, reviving the discussion around embodied cognition. Investigating neonates in the incubator through movement, and the relationship between movement and cognitive development, shows us that embodied cognition is something innately linked to human development.

Learning from this controlled environment could lead to a significant breakthrough for our experience in the metaverse but, more importantly, to the revival of music and music-based therapies and interventions as a means of understanding our emotions, behaviour and cognition at the crossroads of artificial intelligence.

Before we translate this into a digital space, we have to first immerse ourselves in the physical world, understanding what the arts and music bring to it, how they influence our thinking and our behaviour. We do not need to turn our backs on technological evolution, but neither should we take it for granted, as it is our innate ability to be creative and to improvise that will allow for the next leap in the evolution of human knowledge and intelligence.

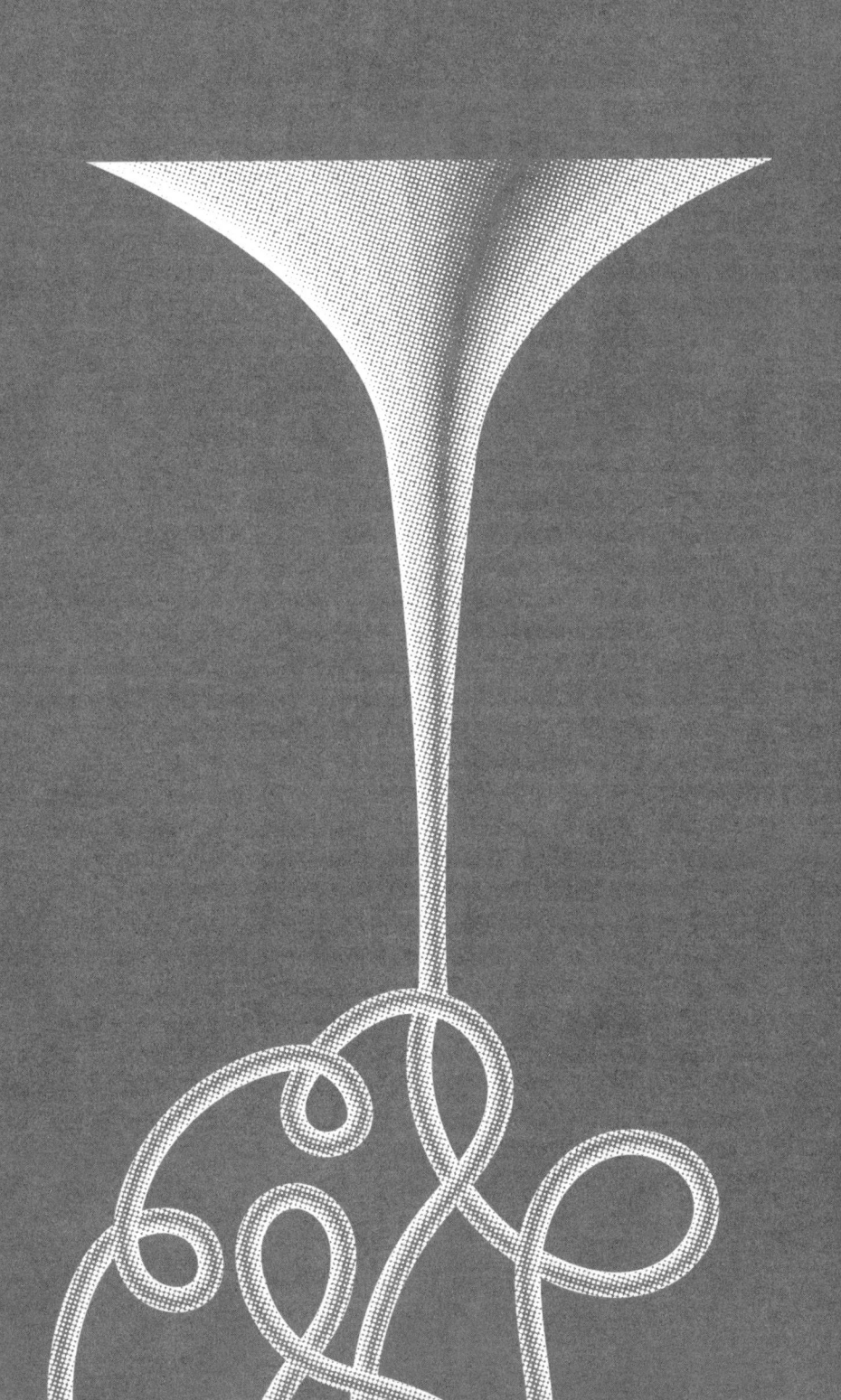

CODA

Since when has the appreciation of beauty become a matter of the brain? Biologically speaking, it always has been, taking the neurosciences, psychology and the hard sciences overall into account.

And yet, when we perceive beauty it is seemingly not our mind, nor brain, that is triggered, but rather feelings or associated emotions connected with our heart, and even sensations in the body. One can of course say that the heart and body are subject to the brain, as the brain controls both heart and body.

The notion of heart versus brain as dualism was posited by Rene Descartes in the eighteenth century; yet despite all the studies since published on the subject, we still do not know whether the body controls the mind, or the mind controls the body. It might well be a combination of the two or neither. We are still searching for the entity that explains human constructs, such as aesthetics, beauty, the arts and, in particular, music. Maybe we have just forgotten how to *think* with our hearts? It seems these days that we cannot really talk about music without talking about the brain. And even though there is a lot of merit in understanding the brain in the context of the perception, processing and execution of music, there is another side to it which we seem to simply forget: following our desire to enjoy, unconditionally, without countless accounts of effectivity or even affectivity. Music undoubtedly triggers certain fine fibres in the brain, supporting neural development and influencing cognition, emotion and behaviour, but perhaps we have elevated it above its central meaning, which is that music is a thing of beauty.

"Not everything that can be counted counts, and not everything that counts can be counted" (attributed to Albert Einstein), and even though we are using music in healthcare and research in humans and the humanities, we need to take a step back and learn to appreciate music again for its simplicity, its beauty and aesthetics.

Our journey, however, has been clouded by our own general belief that science holds all truth and the truths it seeks to find. Science, as we understand it, has searched for the truth by endlessly reducing the subject to its ever-smaller parts, often losing sight of the bigger picture and the context within which the scientific truth will and can operate. As a result, scientists and maybe even many of those who listen to music have reduced it to a product we 'consume'. We devour it as easily as all the other overwhelmingly large amounts of things we fill our lives with, common to wealthy and often Western societies. We carry knowledge and music in our pockets. All the music in the world is at our fingertips, available at any given moment in time, whenever we wish to connect with its soothing, enabling, appealing and stimulating sounds. Its availability in reaching humans may be the reason we are able to classify and research music from a cognitive or neuroscientific point of view. We have reduced it to a luxury product, which belongs to us, as we can control it whenever we wish.

And yet, for some of us, every inch of our mind, body and brain will revolt at such a statement. We revolt because we experience music as being more than simply "auditory cheesecake", as cognitive scientist Steven Pinker famously wrote in his book *How The Mind Works* (1997: 528). We feel, experience, share and enjoy music regardless of its multitude of uses. Music touches us; it touches us quite literally.

In this book we have looked at the different theories which contribute to our understanding of music. However, we are still looking for the ultimate answer to what music really is and, therefore, what are its different uses and meanings. We have identified it as an agent of social interaction or identification, such as the desire to be part of a group which enjoys a certain genre of music and the whole lifestyle identified with that, for example, hip hop, heavy metal or even classical music. All of these different genres come with an external representation in terms of clothing or social environment.

Milton Babbitt (1916–2011), one of America's leading composers, categorised musical phenomena into three different domains: the acoustic or physical, the auditory or perceived, and the graphemic or notated. With these representations of music, Babbitt opened a Pandora's box in trying to understand the different facets of music, as none of the described domains encompass music in all its beauty. In the years since 1960, our comprehension of music as a cognitive representation has fundamentally changed and has been defined as music and musicality, emphasising a general (human) interest in music. A complex stimulus, such as music, consists of different layers. In a physical sense it consists of waves, which are the key to understanding frequencies. Tracing this representation of music back to its origins, we arrived at the beginning of time, at the beginning of the cosmos itself. It was around 13.8 billion years ago when wavelengths, particles and subsequent atoms were first formed, all of which contribute to a physical representation of sound. In the end, sound, and therefore music, is nothing more or less than waves travelling through space, with different frequencies and amplitudes touching our ear drums. It is the organisation of sound, of waves and frequencies, which has allowed the music to be understood by our brains, as well as our physiological reactions to it. The organisation of frequencies, regardless of tonality or atonality, are therefore perceived and encompass every sonic wave, i.e., rhythm, pitch, melody, timbre and harmony.

We have seen that music is made from different building blocks and as soon as it touches our eardrum, quite literally, multiple brain areas and networks are triggered. The sound waves travelling through air touch our ear drums and make them vibrate, translating a mechanical signal into an electrical one, which in turn can be interpreted by the brain as sound. Based on scientific, psychological and cognitive theories, there are two major hypotheses attempting to explain the musical stimulus in the brain. We have explored the resource-sharing hypothesis and the modularity hypothesis, as coined by Anirud Patel and Isabela Peretz, respectively. In Patel's resource-sharing framework, he argued that all perceived auditory information, for example, language or music, shares the same neural networks. Peretz, on the contrary, has argued in her modularity hypothesis that auditory information must have different neural foundations to language and therefore uses different parts of the brain. There is merit in both theories as they both posit that music is a complex stimulus; however, at this early stage in the process we can ponder, as did Stravinsky, whether there is any meaning to music at all without a human agent to interpret it. Language carries meaning in the different conventions we have agreed upon since the first 'hmmmm'. But music seems to be different. Everybody can enjoy and listen to music but even though we agree that we are hearing music, each and every one of us will individually interpret it differently, thus perceiving the music differently. There is no unanimous way of saying a particular piece of music makes everybody happy or everybody sad or everybody laugh. To perceive music, we have to see resource sharing as stage one of perception, and the modularity hypothesis as stage two when perceiving and processing an auditory stimulus. The neuroanatomical actuality is the connectivity to and from the thalamus, the initial interpretation structure, and cortical relays, as part of the evolutionary 'oldest' area of the brain—the brainstem, thalamus and limbic system. Through the centuries, the thalamus has only been regarded as a relay station of incoming sensory information. Recent research[28], however, suggests that it is more than a relay station and thus contributes a great deal to our perception, processing and understanding of the world and everything within it by being strongly and directly connected to areas associated with decision-making, memory, emotions, planning, inhibition and empathy.

When sound or music is sent to the ear, the cochlea relays this information through the brain stem, touching all the nerves, on its way to the thalamus and primary auditory cortex. This process is extremely complex, and we have not yet investigated how the brain makes sense of it all and identifies the incoming stimulus as music. What we do know is that music listening and playing is a 'global cerebral process', utilising the frontal lobe, parietal lobe, occipital lobe, temporal lobe and structures in the basal ganglia cerebellum and brain stem. Each brain area is involved in multiple tasks and only through their connection to one another, as well as to the whole intricate network of multiple areas, can the brain make music out of the symphony of electrical signals representing emotions, memory, feelings, cognitive functions, breathing and moving. All these areas are activated simultaneously, exchanging information with each other as soon as air molecules, in the form of waves, reach our ear, and interpreted as music by our brain and body.

However, more experimental studies are needed to analyse the individual building blocks of the thalamic nuclei, the involved brain networks, their relationship with cognition, behaviour and emotion, and how they link to melody, rhythm, timbre, beat, tone, tonal relationships, intensity and orchestration.

Imagine that all musicians playing in an orchestra are connected with thousands of wires, through which, even though they are not speaking to each other, are exchanging signals in all hidden ways (as musicians in an ensemble do), to create a unified sound out of the cacophony of the individual parts. The mapping in our brain works similar to this, with signals traveling back and forth in-between, with a conductor [the thalamus] holding it together. (Gerald Edelman, 2000:132)

Regarding the interpretation of music, we discussed four principles: 1) passive listening, 2) active listening, 3) music making, and 4) improvisation, all of which recruit networks and areas consecutively building upon each other. Passive listening represents hearing music in the background without 'consciously' being aware of it playing, e.g., sitting in a restaurant talking to your partner with music in the background. We do not focus on it, as we do not focus on the different voices at the other tables, until the moment we hear or recognise a song. Then our conversation stops, our attention is directed towards the song being played, and maybe our conversation turns to an associated memory we might have. We suddenly remember our last trip to Rome, the moment in which we stared up at the ceiling of the Sistine Chapel while the organ played *Toccata and Fugue in* D *Minor* by Bach. Or the memory of the last sunset we witnessed while John Coltrane was enchanting us with his *A Love Supreme*. It is a small step from passive to active listening when it comes to neural activation; however, it can have a large impact on our behaviour, from being completely oblivious to it to being completely immersed in it. To activate even more areas of this neural network, we then decide to leave the restaurant and rush home to play either of the songs just heard, engaging in a shared experience of memory, emotion and togetherness as we play music deep into the night. During this time, we can even leave the safe havens of pre-composed music, improvising around the great compositions of Bach and Coltrane to create something completely new. It is the activation of whole networks involved in perception, processing, production and reorganisation, calling upon different cognitive functions, emotional representations, memory formation and retrieval movement and behaviour, which makes us play an instrument or lets us sing. It is at this stage the two Titans meet: on the one hand, the complex stimulus of music, with all its different dimensions, and on the other, the brain, with all its complex connections and networks, activated by, yet again, another complex stimulus. Maybe it is this meeting which makes music so special in the arts. It touches us, it triggers us, it evokes memories and it brings us back to moments in time we may even have forgotten. As humans we are adept at using music to regulate our emotions. We are the only animal who knows exactly what music to put on when we are determined to make ourselves feel even more miserable.

Using a complex stimulus such as music in different settings—at home, at a festival, in a care home, a hospital or even an intensive care unit—may be the key to why music can be such an effective tool in treatments, healthcare and overall well-being.

There is a general need to amalgamate the neural, psychosocial and clinical aspects and influences of music in healthcare. How music-based therapies and interventions can be protocolised, implemented and assessed in clinical populations is particularly important. Clinical neuroscience offers methodological access to study social interaction processes in therapeutic domains by blending the richness, ecological validity, and contextual factors of real-world designs. Demand is increasing to integrate neuroscience, musicology, the digital humanities, medicine, healthcare therapies and augmented artificial human intelligence. This, in turn, will increasingly utilise big data and artificial intelligence algorithms to analyse neural and physical data related to biomarkers in therapeutic and clinical settings. This means operating on the edge between biomarkers and digital markers. Consequently, this book has focused on the utilisation of proven, as well as new and innovative, methodologies and technologies in music-based therapies and interventions for clinical populations. To understand the impact music and music-based therapies can have on the human mind and body, one has to comprehend the very early stages of both music and human life itself, including our understanding of the foetal period and very early childhood.

*

Music and its relationship to neuromusicology, and in turn the physiology of the human body, has been researched in many ways throughout the years. The discourse on combining systematic, historical and cognitive musicology has been one of the key areas of discussion in cross-domain music. For example, anthropologists consider the cultural background, which appears to serve as one candidate in the understanding of music making; however, fields such as cognitive science and neuroscience do not seem to regard these influences as primary to the results of their research. One cannot study brain functions while making music without considering the socio-cultural backgrounds in which the musician learned to play and where the music-making is taking place, or the parameters of generally acquiring musical skills. Thus, speaking of experiencing music, and therefore listening to it through experienced and conscious representations, it must be analysed with both the ontological and epistemological approach in mind. The ontological concerns the very nature of the social world investigated. It poses the question of existence or reality from a philosophical view. The epistemological approach refers to the 'grounds of knowledge', i.e., what is knowledge, how do we acquire knowledge, and how do we know what we know.

According to philosopher Alexander Douglas, it is of paramount importance to develop a "new lens" to understand a collective phenomenology of music. We have to search for the underlying critical anthropology instead of a collective philosophy, which will allow for a broader view of how we experience music and, in turn, will shine light on the conundrum of translating music into the digital realm, i.e., allowing an artificial intelligence to create and improvise music as humans would. One has to approach this problem from the ground up: first, understanding the anthropological and epistemological dialogue of what music means to us as humans and, second, how this translates to cognitive functioning, emotion and behaviour in the moment of experiencing music.

A reasonable basic ontological concept of music making would not distinguish between a) a free improvisation at a music festival; b) a doxological gathering of a group of Sufi in the North African desert; c) [...] a group of undergraduates simply rehearsing a Mahler symphony 'just because' and d) a rendition of a favoured song in the shower. (Douglas, 2018:20)

All four are indeed instances of music making, but all have different social, cognitive, emotional and behavioural backgrounds and therefore the interpretation of each of these musical experiences is different. According to Douglas, a) is a performance, b) a religious ceremony, c) a gathering without an audience, and d) a private matter. And yet they are all linked through an active musical experience. Dissecting this issue, one can clearly see the music aspect running through all of them; however, this does not make the picture complete as we also have to take the context into consideration. Here we find ourselves at the crossroads between intelligence and consciousness, between possibly *brain versus heart*. As humans, we will easily understand each of the above musical experiences for what they are, i.e., a performance or religious ceremony. This understanding comes from our built-in musical baggage, our associations with memory and emotions, and the context of these experiences. We therefore do not only perceive the world around us and thus exist, but we also experience it through different aspects, fitting into a contextual bubble depending on the experience.

Try to translate this into an artificial intelligence algorithm; the machine will not understand the different contexts of the above four examples unless we programme it to identify exactly just these. However, this does not mean that the machine cannot learn; yet considering the sheer variety of different ways of making music and therefore experiencing it to its fullest, with all its different social, cultural and emotional meanings, it allows for a sheer infinite number of musical experiences.

*

Sometimes we have to jump into the deep end to understand such a complex stimulus as music, something we thought as impossible at the start of our endeavour. Sometimes we must take a long look in the mirror, reflect, and realise that we have more abilities than we thought we did. Improvisation is one of those abilities. Through millennia of evolution, our brains have been adapted by our ability to improvise. The ever-growing networks of synapses and neurons have made us who we are as humans. Our ability to improvise has contributed a great deal to this development. It is about the freedom to choose freedom that allows us to dig up ideas that we never dreamt of conjuring up. This innate ability does not only allow us to think for ourselves and create something out of thin air, but it also translates into the way we interact with others, in conversation, in therapy or in the digital realm. The crossroads between mind and body is key to understanding our interaction with the world and must be cherished from the very start of our lives. Whether we can create a safer environment for neonates in incubators, or challenge our brain with new activities, such as learning a language or reading a good book, all of these contribute to the way we think creatively and improvise in search of beauty, order and chaos. Beauty lies in the ear of the improviser; your brain is ready—are you?

ENDNOTES

1   [...] *we might have just been paying the price for not having taken scientific research seriously enough.* Yuval Noah Harari stated this in an interview with the *Guardian* in 2021.

2   *New normality;* this term has been used throughout the media in the context of a new normal post COVID, implying that everything is as it was before the pandemic.

3   *Neurolinguistic Programming* is an approach to communication and influence through communication on development, preferences and memory and was first described by Edward Berneys in the 1930s. The term, as understood today, first appeared in *The Structure of Magic*, Bandler & Grinder, 1975.

4   [...] *awoke one morning with the not too unbelievable futuristic fantasy that one day we would be able to enter our smart kitchens where robots would make us coffee and fry an egg for us. In this future, we would be driven to work by smart cars while we relaxed behind the wheel and read a newspaper.* Jacob Nelson has elaborated on this in his online piece *Is technology making us lazy?*, 2017, https://medium.com/digital-society/is-technology-making-us-lazy-ec3a3e58140a

5   *Groundhog Day*, Director Harold Ramis, 1993, Columbia Pictures.

6   [...] *writes mockingly that today's scouts need to learn how to use* GPS-*technology instead of a compass. Jackson argues that with every new technological invention, we become less active, both physically and*

cognitively, and that therefore we are becoming increasingly dependent on a screen, and he worries that one day we will become like those humans in the animation movie Wall-E, who spend their days lounging in chairs—the epitome of laziness. Dominique Jackson argued this in his online article *Has Technology Made us Lazy and Dependent?*, 2017, https://www.lifehack.org/articles/technology/has-technology-made-lazy-and-dependent.html

7   *"So far there has been no emotion transmitted, no understanding of harmony or meaning."* Igor Stravinsky was a vehement advocate of no emotions in music. He used this expression on multiple occasions, making it difficult to trace to the original written source. Most likely, he used the expression in conversation to reinforce his stance that music has to happen in a (specific) context. *Igor Stravinsky, An Autobiography* (2008), Baltzell Press.

8   *The diversity of cognitive and behavioural processes underlying such appreciation must therefore be rooted in human epigenetics, as it seems to be such a universal human trait.* Researcher and professor of Music Cognition Henkjan Honing has spent a significant amount of time researching this phenomenon

9   *The hmmmmm:* our knowledge about the development of music and language is based on the work of different disciplines encompassing anthropology, musicology, neuroscience, psychology, history and archaeology.

10   [...] *this is an often-overlooked fact, they leave an immense CO_2 footprint and are one of the biggest contributors to global warming with all their data centres running 24/7 ".* Recent discussion in science, politics and media, indicate that one of the biggest contributors to CO_2 emissions are data centres and, moreover, the owner-greedy need to have everything available 24/7 to satisfy our streaming needs.

11   *Mind the Music Playlist:* Link and code at the end of the book.

12   *Franz Josef Gall (1758–1828)* was a German neuroanatomist,
      physiologist and pioneer in bringing together mental function and
      anatomical brain structures

13   *Today most orchestras use the agreed standard reference pitch of 440
      Hz; however, there are also the odd ones out, who believe that an
      alternative pitch contributes to their particular sound, like the New
      York Philharmonic, the Boston Symphony Orchestra or the Dutch
      Royal Concertgebouw Orchestra, who all tune in A = 442 Hz. German
      orchestras often tune in 443 Hz, the Lithuanian Chamber Orchestra
      in Wilnus uses 444 Hz and the English Baroque Soloists a tuning of
      A = 430 Hz. Which frequency is the best lies in the ear of the listener.*
      This information was gathered from the individual homepages of
      the orchestras in 2023.

14   • *Sruti:* The smallest interval used. It is considered the single most
      important element of Indian music.
      • *Svara:* is regarded as the central point around which melodic
      activity takes place. It stands in a 'non-harmonic' relationship to
      the *sruti.*
      • *Tala:* Rhythmic cycle of the second part of the raga with
      variations of fixed lengths, e.g., 16, 12 or 8 matra.
      • *Laya:* The pulse of the music. It is regarded as the forward
      motion, the feel, of the rhythm.
      • *Raga:* is the framework of the whole piece and the context
      of improvisation of the musicians. It is unformed until the
      performance.
      • *Alapa:* The slow introduction to the *raga.*
      • *Gat:* Treatment of the *raga* in various standard ways.

15   *Ray Kurzweil's Singularity:* Author and scientist, Kurzweil has
      written that in technology, singularity describes the point of no

return, when technology has outgrown humans irreversibly. These intelligent and powerful technologies will take over every aspect of human life and radically alter and transform our reality. Kurzweil, 2006, *The Singularity is Near.*

16   *"we ran out of pitta, you want Hovis?"* All credit to Alexei Sayle for this wonderful sketch. BBC Radio.

17   [...] *there are so many different solos and tunes out there that it is nearly impossible to choose the wrong notes or tunes to play in any given context.* Joshua Redman during a performance and lecture on jazz improvisation at the Juilliard School, New York, 2010.

18   *"well, man, this is what I feel like playing; it is a very structured thing that comes down from a tradition and requires a lot of thought and study."* Wynton Marsalis in Paul F. Berliner, 1994, *Thinking Jazz.*

19   [...] *time as a superstring and reducing it to gravity alone* [...]. The idea of time and gravity as superstrings comes from nuclear physics and astrophysics: it means that you can reduce time into matter, matter into particles, and particles into one never-ending string that reduces itself again to gravity, which becomes only mass. Imagine the weight of the whole earth flattened to one infinitely long string with only a thousandth of a millimetre thickness.

20   [...] *get into the zone, into the so-called runner's high.* Boecker et al., 2009, "The runner's high: opioidergic mechanisms in the human brain," Cerebral Cortex, 18(11): 2523–31.

21   [...] *tonic* (I), *dominant* (v) *and subdominant* (IV) *as the most stable chords*: Each note of a scale has a special name, called a scale degree. The first (and last note is called the tonic. The fifth note is

called the dominant and the fourth note is called the subdominant, regardless of the key.

22   *Schrödinger's Cat.* In Schrödinger's original formulation, a cat, a flask of poison, and a radioactive source are placed in a sealed box. If an internal monitor (e.g., a Geiger counter) detects radioactivity (i.e., a single atom decaying), the flask is shattered, releasing the poison, which kills the cat. The Copenhagen interpretation implies that, after a while, the cat is *simultaneously* alive *and* dead. Yet, when one looks in the box, one sees the cat *either* alive *or* dead, not both alive *and* dead. This poses the question of when exactly quantum superposition ends and reality resolves into one possibility or the other. Wikipedia 06/2023 https://en.wikipedia.org/wiki/Schr%C3%B6dinger%27s_cat

23   *"Neurons that fire and Neurons that Fire."* Donald Hebb used this famous phrase throughout his career, which has become a mantra for neuroscientists.

24   *"If a cluttered desk is a sign of a cluttered mind, of what, then, is an empty desk a sign of?"* There is no date or publication outlet for this quote, however it has been associated with Einstein.

25   *"How are we going to make sense out of this?"* Bassist Dave Holland's comment upon arrival at the recording session to Miles Davis's album *Bitches Brew* (1969).

26   Nick Cave reacted to ChatGPT writing a song in his style. The prompt was first published online, and shared with Nick Cave, who reacted to the lyrics: https://www.theredhandfiles.com/chat-gpt-what-do-you-think/ (January 2023). Their exchange was later published in the Guardian (UK); https://www.theguardian.com/music/2023/jan/17/this-song-sucks-nick-cave-responds-to-chatgpt-song-written-in-style-of-nick-cave (January 2023).

27   Erik Elliot in Emil Angerval (2022) online article. *Music to grow body in metaverse, start new age of connection and immersion*: https://cryptoslate.com/music-to-grow-body-in-metaverse-start-new-age-of-connection-and-immersion/

28   *recent research* on the effects of music therapy in the NICU, van Dokkum et al., 2020; Bos et al., 2021; Span et al., 2021; Kraft et al., 2021; Ormston et al., 2022; Jaschke & Bos, 2023.

REFERENCES

Adelman, G., & Smith, B. H., eds. (1999), *Encyclopaedia of Neuroscience*, vols. I & II, Amsterdam, Lausanne, New York, Oxford, Shannon, Singapore & Tokyo: Elsevier.

Aiello, R., & Sloboda, J. A., eds. (1994), *Musical Perception*, New York & Oxford: Oxford University Press.

Alluri, V., Toiviainen, P., Jääskeläinen, I. P., Glerean, E., Sams, M., & Brattico, E. (2012), "Large-scale brain networks emerge from dynamic processing of musical timbre, key and rhythm," *NeuroImage* 59: 3677–89.

Altenmüller, E., & Schlaug, G. (2012), "Music, Brain and Health: Exploring Biological Foundations of Music's Health Effects," in MacDonald, Kreutz & Mitchell, eds., *Music Health and Wellbeing*, Oxford & New York: Oxford University Press.

Altenmueller, E. (2003), "Focal dystonia: Advances in brain imaging and understanding of fine motor control in musicians," *Hand Clinics* 19: 1–16.

Altenmueller, E. (2010), "The musician's brain as a model for adaptive and maladaptive plasticity," in F. C. Rose, ed., *The Neurology of Music*, London: Imperial College Press.

Althusler, I. M. (1944), "Four years of experience with music as a therapeutic agent at Eloise Hospital," *American Journal of Psychiatry* 100(7): 792–94.

Alperson, P. (1984), "On musical improvisation," *Journal of Aesthetics and Art Criticism* 43: 17–29.

Andrade, P. E., Vanzella, P., Andrade, O. V. C. A., & Schellenberg, E. G. (2017), "Associating emotions with Wagner's music: A developmental perspective," *Psychology of Music* 45(5): 752–60.

AMTA (American Music Therapy Association, no date) https://www. musictherapy.org/about/quotes/definition. Accessed 05/02/2019.

Atkinson, R. C., & Shiffrin, R. M. (1968), "Human Memory: a proposed system and its control processes," in Spence and Spence, eds, *The Psychology of Learning and Motivation*, 2nd ed., New York: Academic Press.

Babbitt, M. (1965), "The use of computers in musicological research," *Perspectives of New Music* 3(2): 74–83.

Bailey, D. (1992), *Musical Improvisation: Its Nature and Practice in Music*, Ashbourne, Eng. & Englewood Cliffs, New Jersey: Practise Hall.

Baker, D. (1969), *Jazz Improvisation*, Chicago: Maher.

Ball, P. (2010), *The Music Instinct: How music works and why we can't do without it*, London: The Bodley Head.

Balliett, W. (1977), *Improvising*, New York: Oxford University Press.

Barraud, Q., & Berthet, A. (2009), "Direct projection from the subthalamic nucleus to the thalamus in the primate model of PD," PD online research.

Baroni, M. (2010), "GTTM and post-tonal music," *Musicae Scientiae, Discussion Forum* 5: 69–93.

Beech, A., (2013), "Science and its fiction," notes from a talk on scientific method, California Institute of the Arts, private communication, Valencia, CA.

Bengsston, S. L., Csikszentmihalyi, M., & Ullen, F. (2007), "Advacnes of Music and Meuroscince, in F. Clifford Rose, ed., *The Neurology of Music*, London: Imperial College Press.

Benson, B. E. (2009), *The Improvisation of Musical Dialogue: A Phenomenology of Music*, Cambridge & New York: Cambridge University Press.

Benward, B., & Wildman, J. (1984), *Jazz Improvisation in Theory and Practice*, Dubuque, Iowa: Wm. C. Brown.

Berendt, J.-E. (1989), *Das Jazz Buch*, 7th ed., Frankfurt: S. Fischer Verlag.

Bergen, van, A. (2007), "Freedom and limits of jazz improvisation," *Journal of the Indian Musicological Society* 38: 36–43, Mumbai India.

Berkowitz, A. L. (2009), *The Improvising Mind, Cognition and Creativity in the Musical Moment*, New York: Oxford University Press.

Berliner, P. F. (1994), *Thinking in Jazz: The Infinite Art of Improvisation*, Chicago & London: University of Chicago Press.

Bernays, E. (1947), *The Engineering of Consent*, Oklahoma: University of Oklahoma Press.

Bharucha, J. J. (1984), "Anchoring effects in music: The resolution of dissonance," *Cognitive Psychology* 16: 485–518.

Bharucha, J. J. (1984), "Event hierarchies, tonal hierarchies and assimilation: A reply to Deutsch and Dowling," *Journal of Experimental Psychology* 113: 421–25.

Bharucha, J. J. (1996), "Melodic Anchoring," *Music Perception* 13(3): 383–400.

Bharucha, J. J., & Krumhansl, C. L. (1983), "The representation of harmonic structure in music: Hierarchies of stability as a function of context," *Cognition* 13: 63–102.

Blacking, J. (1973), *How Musical is Man?* Seattle & London: University of Washington Press.

Blood, A. J., & Zatorre, R. J. (2001), "Intensely pleasurable responses to music correlate with activity in brain regions implicated in reward and emotions," *Proceedings of the National Academy of Science* 98, 11818–23.

Blumenfeld, H. (2010), *Neuroanatomy through Clinical Cases*, 2nd ed., Sunderland, Massachusetts: Sinauer Associates Publishers.

Bonath, B., Tyll, S., Budinger, E., Krauel, K., Hopf, J.-M., & Noesselt, T. (2013), "Task-demands and audio-visual stimulus configurations modulate neural activity in the human thalamus," *NeuroImage* 66(2): 110–18.

Bos, M., van Dokkum, N. H., Ravensbergen, A. G., Kraft, K. E., Bos, F., Jaschke, A. C. (2021), "Pilot study finds that performing live music therapy in intensive care units may be beneficial for infants' neurodevelopment," *Acta Paediatrica*, online.

Brown, J. C. (1992), "Musical fundamental frequency tracking using a pattern recognition method," *Journal of the Acoustical Society of America* 92:1394.

Burrell, G., & Morgan, G. (1979), *Sociological Paradigms and Organisational Analysis*, London: Heinemann.

Burns, K. (2000), *Jazz: A Film by Ken Burns*, DVD, PBS Home Video.

Cabeza, R., & Kingstone, A. (2006), *Handbook of Functional Neuroimaging of Cognition*, 2nd ed., Cambridge, MA & London: MIT Press.

Canbor, G. C., Lisowitz, G. M., & Miller, M. D. (no date), "Creative jazz musicians: A clinical study," *Psychiatry* 25(1): 1–15.

Cappe, C., Morel, A., Barone, P., & Rouiller, E. M. (2009), "The thalamocortical projection systems in primates: An anatomical support for multisensory and sensorimotor integrations," *Cerebral Cortex* 19: 2025–37.

Cappe, C., Rouiller, E. M., & Barone, P. (2012), "Cortical and Thalamic Pathways for Multisensory and Sensorimotor Interplay," chapter 2 in M. M. Murray & M. T. Wallace, eds., *The Neural Basis of Multisensory Processes*, Boca Raton: CRC Press.

Chalmers, D. (1998), "The Extended Mind," *Analysis* 58(1): 7–19.

Crowe, B. J., & Rio, R. (2004), "Implications of music technology in music therapy practice and research for music therapy education: A review of literature," *Journal of Music Therapy* 41(4): 282–320.

Clifton, T. (1983), *Music as Heard: A Study in Applied Phenomenology*, New Haven, CN: Yale University Press.

Clynes, M. (1982), *Music Mind and Brain: The Neuropsychology of Music*, New York & London: Plenum Press.

Coher, J. (1964), *Improvising Jazz*, Englewood Cliffs, NJ: Prentice-Hall.

Coltrane, J. (1960), *The Avant-Garde*, Record label Impulse!

Coltrane, J. (1965), *A Love Supreme*, Record label Impulse!

Coltrane, J. (1966), *Ascensions*, Record label Impulse!

Corrigall, A., Schellenberg, E. G., & Misura, N. M. (2013), "Music training, cognition and personality," *Front Psychology* 4: 222.

Cowan, N. (1988), "Evolving conceptions of memory storage, selective attention, and their mutual constraints within the human information processing system," *Psychological Bulletin* 104(2): 163–91.

De Graaf, T. (2016), *Onderzoek met Impact, Strategische Onderzoeksagenda*, HBO 2016–20.

Dauer, A. M. (1960), "Improvisation: zur Technik der spontanen Gestaltung in Jazz," *JazzForschung/JazzResearch* 1: 113–32.

Deutsch, D., ed. (1999), *The Psychology of Music*, 2nd ed., San Diago: Academic Press.

DeVeaux, S. (1998), "Constructing the Jazz tradition," *Journal of the American Musicological Society* 51(2): 392–406; California: University of California Press.

Dreu, M. J., van der Wilk, A. S. D., Poppe, E., Kwakkel, G., & van Wegen, E. E. H. (2012), "Rehabilitation, exercise therapy and music in patients with Parkinson's disease: a meta-analysis of the effects of music-based movement therapy on walking ability, balance and quality of life," *Parkinsonism & Related Disorders* 18(1): 114–19.

Douglas, A. (2018), "Music, Language and Mental Health: Music as Epistemic Necessity," in Williams, Waddington-Jones, Mawby & Sharpe, eds., *Music, Mental Health & Wellbeing*, 2019, vol. 1; *Musicological Research Journal* 6.

Dowling, W. J. (1978), "Scale and contour: two components of a theory of memory for melodies," *Psychological Review* 85: 341–54.

Dowling, W. J., & Fujitani, D. S. (1971), "Contour, interval and pitch recognition in memory for melodies," *Journal of the Acoustic Society of America* 49: 524–31.

Edelman, G. M. (1978), *Neural Darwinism: The theory of Neural Group Selection*, Basic Books.

Edelman, G. M. (2000), "In our Time Imagination and Consciousness," BBC Radio 4, 29 June.

Edwards, J. (2016), "Approaches and models of music therapy," in J. Edwards, ed., *The Oxford Handbook of Music Therapy*, pp. 417–27, Oxford: Oxford University Press.

Einstein, A. (1917), letter to Felix Klein, "On determinism and approximations," quoted in *Pais* (1982), chapter 17.

Engel, A., & Keller, P. E. (2011), "The perception of musical spontaneity in improvised and imitated jazz performances," *Frontiers in Psychology* 2(83): 1–13.

Epstein, J. M. (1996), *Growing Artificial Societies: Social Science from the bottom up (Complex Adaptive Systems)*, Cambridge, MA: MIT Press.

Eysenck, M. W., & Keane, M. T. (2005), *Cognitive Psychology: A Student's Handbook*, 5th ed., East Sussex: Psychology Press.

Fachner, J. C., Maidhof, C., Grocke, D., Nygaard Pedersen, I., Rondalen, G., Tucek, G., & Bonde, L. O. (2019), "'Telling me not to worry…' Hyperscanning and Neural Dynamics of Emotion Processing during Guided Imagery and Music," *Frontiers in Psychology* 10.

Feynman, R. P. (1995), *Six Easy Pieces*, Reading, MA: Addison-Wesley Pub. Co.

Fletcher, P. C., Firth, C. D., Grasby, P. M., Shallice, T., Frackowiak, R. S. J., & Dolan, R. J. (1994), "Brain systems for encoding and retrieval of auditory-verbal memory," an in vivo study in humans, open source article.

Forde Thomson, W. (2009), *Music, Thought, and Feeling: Understanding the Psychology of Music*, New York & Oxford: Oxford University Press.

Grasby, P. M., Firth, C. D., Friston, K. J., Bench, C., Frackowiak, R. S. J., & Dolan, R. J. (1992), "Functional mapping of brain areas implicated in auditory-verbal memory function," open source article.

Gepner, B., & Feron, F. (2009), "Autism: A world changing too fast for a mis-wired brain?" *Neuroscience and Biobehavioural Reviews* 33: 1227–42.

Gibson, J. J. (1979), *The Ecological Approach to Visual Perception*, Boston, MA: Houghton Mifflin.

Gied, J. N. (2012), "The Digital Revolution and Adolescent Brain Evolution," *Journal of Adolescent Health* 51(2): 101–05.

Graham, P. (2001), *Phrenology: Revealing the mysteries of the mind*, Richmond Hill: American Home Treasures.

Greenwood, P. M., & Parasuraman, R. (2016), "The mechanisms of far transfer from cognitive training: review and hypothesis," *Neuropsychology* 30(6): 742–55.

Hahna, N. D., et al. (2012), "Music technology usage in music therapy: A survey of practice," *Arts in Psychotherapy* 39(5): 456–64.

Hall, B. (1999), *Consciousness: How the Brain makes sense of it all*, New York: Routledge.

Hall, E. T. (1992), "Improvisation as an acquired, multilevel process," *Ethnomusicology* 36(2): 223–35.

Hamilton, A. (2000), "The art of improvisation and the aesthetics of imperfection," *British Journal of Aesthetics* 40(1): 168–85.

Harris, S. (2010), *The Moral Landscape: How human sciences can define human values*, New York: Free Press.

Hawking, S., "Gödel and the end of physics," lecture at the Wayback Machine, 20 July 2002.

Haynes, J. D., & Rees, G. (2006), "Decoding mental states from brain activity in humans," *Nature Reviews in Neuroscience* 7: 523–34.

Haynes, J. D., Soon, C. S., Brass, M., & Heinze, H.-J. (2008), "Unconscious determinants of free decisions in the human brain," *Nature Neuroscience* 11: 543–45.

Hickok, G., Buchsbaum, B., Humphries, C., & Muftuler, T. (2003), "Auditory-motor interaction revealed by fMRI: speech, music and working memory in area Spt," *Journal of Cognitive Neuroscience* 15(5), 673–82.

Honing, H. (2018), *The Origins of Musicality*, Cambridge, MA: MIT Press.

Honing, H., ten Cate, C., Peretz, I., & Trehub, S. (2015), "Without it no music: cognition, biology, and evolution of musicality." *Philosophical Transactions of the Royal Society B: Biological Sciences* 370.

Horden, P., ed. (2016), *Music and Medicine: The history of music therapy since antiquity*, New York, NY/Oxon: Routledge.

Huron, D. (2006), *Sweet Anticipation: Music and the Psychology of Expectation*, Cambridge, MA: MIT Press.

Huron, D., & Hellmuth Margulis, E. (2009), "Musical Expectancy and Thrills," in P. N. Juslin & J. Sloboda, eds., *Music and Emotion*, New York: Oxford University Press.

Ito, H. T., Zhang, S. J., Witter, M. P., Moser, E. I., & Moser, M. B. (2015), "A prefrontal–thalamo–hippocampal circuit for goal-directed spatial navigation," *Nature* 522, 50–55.

Jarrett, K. (2005), *The Art of Improvisation*, EuroArts.

Jaschke, A. C., Eggermont, L. H. P., Honing, H., & Scherder, E. J. A. (2013), "Music education and its effect on intellectual abilities in children: a systematic review," *Review of Neuroscience* 24(6): 665–75.

Jaschke, A. C., Honing, H., & Scherder, E. J. A. (2018), "Longitudinal analysis of music education on executive functions in primary school children," *Frontiers in Neuroscience* 12.

Jaschke, A. C. (2019), "Music, Maestro, Please: Multisensory thalamic integration in music perception, processing and production," *Music and Medicine* 11(2).

Jaschke, A. C., & Bos, A. F. (2023), "Concept and Consideration of a Medical Device: The Active Noise Cancelling Incubator," *Frontiers in Pediatrics* 11 – neonatology, technology and code section.

Janata, P. (2009), "The neural architecture of music-evoked autobiographical memories," *Cerebral Cortex* 9(11).

Joyce, B., & Showers, B. (2002), *Student achievement through staff development*, Alexandria, VA: ASCD.

Justus, T. C., & Bharucha, J. J. (2002), "Music perception and cognition," in *Stevens' Handbook of Experimental Psychology*, New York: Wiley, pp. 453–92.

Kahn, U. R. (2010), interview conducted on 13 June 2010.

Kahrs, M., & Brandenburg, K. H. (1998), *Applications of Digital Signal Processing to Audio and Acoustics*, New York, Boston, Dordrecht, London, Moscow: Kluwer Academic Publishers.

Kao, L. S., Tyson, J. E., & Lally, K. P. (2008), "Clinical research methodology I: Introduction to randomized trials," *Journal of the American College of Surgeons* 206(2): 361–69.

Kandel, E. R., Schwartz, J. H., & Jessell, T. M. (1991), *Principles of Neural Science*, 3rd ed., London: Prentice-Hall International Inc.

Kanellopoulos, P. A. (2007), "Musical Improvisation as Action: An Arendtian Perspective," *Action, Criticism and Theory for Musical Education* 6(3): 97–127.

Kay, B. P., Meng, X., DiFrancesco, M. W., Holland, S. K., & Szaflarski, J. P. (2012), "Moderating effects of music on resting state networks," *Brain Research* 1447: 53–64.

Kenrick, D. T., & Butner, J. (2003), *Dynamical Evolutionary Psychology: Individual Decision Rules*, New Jersey: Psychology Press.

Kenrick, D. T. (2011), *Sex, murder and the meaning of life: A psychologist investigates how evolution, cognition and complexity are revolutionizing our view of human nature*, New York: Basic Books.

Klein, C., Liem, F., Hänggi, J., Elmer, S., & Jäncke, L. (2016) "The 'silent' imprint of musical training," *Human Brain Mapping* 37(2).

Kok, M., & Lomber, S. (2017) "Origin of the thalamic projection to dorsal auditory cortex hearing and deafness," *Hearing Research* 343, 108–17.

Konig, R., Heil, P., Budinger, E., & Scheich, H., eds. (2015), *The Auditory Cortex: A synthesis of human and animal research*, Oxford: Psychology Press.

Koelsch, S. (2014), "Brain correlates of music-evoked emotions," *Nature Reviews Neuroscience* 15(3), 170–80.

Kraft, K. E., Jaschke, A. C., Ravensbergen, A. G., Feenstra-Weelink, A., van Goor, M. E. L., de Kroon, M. L. A., Reijneveld, S. A., Bos, A. F., & van Dokkum, N. H. (2021), "Maternal Anxiety, Infant Stress, and the Role of Live-Performed Music Therapy during NICU stay in the Netherlands, *International Journal of Environmental Research and Public Health* 18(13): 7077.

Kraus, N., & Chandrasekaran, B. (2010), "Music training for the development of auditory skills," *Nature Reviews Neuroscience* 11: 599–605.

Krell, C., et al. (2016), *The Digital Society: Impulses for the Digitalisation Congress*, Bonn: Friedrich Ebert Stiftung.

Krumhansl, C. L. (1979), "The psychological representation of musical pitch in a tonal context," *Cognitive Psychology* 11: 346–74.

Krumhansl, C. L. (1990), *Cognitive Foundations of Musical Pitch*, Oxford: Oxford University Press.

Krumhansl, C. L. (1991), "Musical psychology: tonal structures in perception and memory," *Annual Review of Psychology* 42: 277–303.

Krumhansl, C. L. (1995), "Music psychology and music theory: problems and prospects, *Music Theory Spectrum* 17: 173–96.

Krumhansl, C. L. (2000), "Rhythm and pitch in music cognition," *Psychological Bulletin* 126: 159–79.

Krumhansl, C. L., Bharucha, J. J., & Castellano, M. A. (1982), "Key distance effects on perceived harmonic structure in music," *Perception & Psychophysics* 32: 96–108.

Krumhansl, C. L., Bharucha, J. J., & Kessler, E. J. (1982), "Perceived harmonic structure of chords in three related musical keys," *Journal of Experimental Psychology: Human perception and performance* 8: 24–36.

Krumhansl, C. L. & Shepard, R. N. (1979), "Quantification of the hierarchy of tonal functions within a diatonic context," *Journal of Experimental Psychology: Human perception and performance* 5: 579–94.

Kuhn, T. S. (2012), *The Structure of Scientific Revolutions*, 50th anniversary ed., Chicago: University of Chicago Press.

Kurzweil, R. (2006), *The Singularity is Near*, London: Duckworth Books.

Leman, M. (1997), *Music, Gestalt and Computing: Studies in Cognitive and Systematic Musicology*, Berlin: Springer.

Lee, H. L., & Noppeney, U. (2011), "Long-term music training tunes how the brain temporally binds signals from multiple senses," *Proceedings of the National Academy of Sciences* 108(51): 1441–50.

Lee, G., & Kisilevsky, B. (2014), "Fetuses respond to father's voice but prefer mother's voice after birth," *Developmental Psychobiology* 56.

Lerdahl, F., & Jackendoff, R. (1983), *A Generative Theory of Tonal Music*, Cambridge, MA: MIT Press.

Lewis, G. E. (2008), *A Power stronger than itself: The AACM and American Experimental Music*, Chicago & London: University of Chicago Press.

Levitin, D. (2006), *This is your Brain on Music: Understanding a Human Obsession*, London: Atlantic Books.

Limb, C. J., & Braun, A. R. (2008), "Neural substrates of spontaneous musical performance: an fMRI study of jazz improvisation," PLOS One 3: 1–15.

Loewy, J., & Jaschke, A. C. (2020), "Mechanisms of timing, timbre, repertoire, and entrainment in neuroplasticity: mutual interplay in neonatal development," *Frontiers in Integrative Neuroscience* 14.

Loewy, J., Stewart, K., Dassler, A.-M., Telsey, A., & Homel, P. (2013), "The effects of music therapy on 356 vital signs, feeding, and sleep in premature infants," *Pediatrics* 131(5): 902–18.

MacDonald, C., & Henson, R. A. (1977), *Music and the Brain: Studies in the Neurology of Music*, London: William Heinemann Medical Books Limited.

Magee, W. L. (2014), *Music Technology in Therapeutic and Health Settings*, London: Jessica Kingsley.

Magee, W. L., & Stewart, L. (2015), "The challenges and benefits of a genuine partnership between music therapy and neuroscience: a dialog between scientist and therapist," *Frontiers in Human Neuroscience* 9: 223.

McMahon, E., Wintermark, P., Lahav, A. (2012), "Auditory brain development in premature infants: the importance of early experience," *Annals of the New York Academy of Science* 1252: 17–24.

Merleau-Ponty, M. (2007), *The Phenomenology of Perception*, 2nd ed., London & New York: Taylor and Francis.

Meyer, L. B. (1989), *Style and Music: Theory, History and Ideology*, Philadelphia: University of Pennsylvania Press.

Monson, I. (1996), *Saying Something: Jazz Improvisation and Interaction*, Chicago & London: University of Chicago Press.

Montuori, A. (2003), "The complexity of improvisation and the improvisation of complexity: social science, art and creativity," *Human Relations* 56(2): 237–55; London & New Delhi: Sage Publications.

Moorman, D. L. (1984), "An analytical study of jazz improvisation, with suggestions for performance," PhD dissertation, New York University.

Munoz-Lopez, M. M., Mohedano-Moriano, A., & Insausti, R. (2010), "Anatomical pathways for auditory memory in primates," open access article, University of Castilla-La Mancha.

Murphy, G. (2002), *The Big Book of Concepts*, Cambridge, MA: MIT Press.

Musacchia, G., & Schroeder, C. E. (2009), "Neural mechanisms, response dynamics and perceptual functions of multisensory interactions in auditory cortex," *Hearing Research* 258: 72–79.

Murray, M. M., Wallace, M. T., eds. (2012), *The Neural Basis of Multisensory Processes*, Boca Raton: CRC Press.

Miranda, E. R. (2017), "Music, brain waves and digitalisation in society," *Brain Music* 4(3).

Nagler, J. C. (2011), "Music therapy methods with handheld music devices in contemporary clinical practice: a commentary," *Music and Medicine* 3: 196.

Nettl, B. (1974), "Thoughts on Improvisation: A Comparative Approach," *Musical Quarterly* 60(1): 1–19.

Nettl, B. (1991), "New perspectives on improvisational issues," *World of Music* 33(3); Wilhelmshaffen: Florian Noetzel Edition.

Norton, A., Winner, E., Cronin, K., Overy, K., Dennis, J. L., & Schlaug, G. (2005), "Are there pre-existing neural, cognitive, or motoric markers for musical ability?" *Brain and Cognition* 59: 124–34.

Oechslin, M. S., Imfeld, A., Loenneker, T., Meyer, M., & Jäncke, L. (2010), "The plasticity of the superior longitudinal fasciculus as a function of musical expertise: a diffusion tensor imaging study," *Frontiers in Neuroscience* 3: 1–12.

Ormston, K., Howard, R., Gallagher, K., Mitra, S., & Jaschke, A. C. (2022), The Role of Music Therapy with Infants with Perinatal Brain Injury," *Brain Science* 12(5): 578.

Overy, K., Norton, A. C., Cronin, K. T., Gaab, N., Alsop, D. C., Winner, E., & Schlaug, G. (2004), "Imaging melody and rhythm processing in young children," *NeuroReport* 15(11): 1723–26.

Patel, A. D. (2012), "Language, music, and the brain: A resource-sharing framework," in P. Rebuschat, M. Rohrmeier, J. Hawkins & I. Cross, eds., *Language and Music as Cognitive Systems*, pp. 204–23, Oxford: Oxford University Press.

Pereboom, D. (2003), *Living without Free Will*, Cambridge: Cambridge University Press.

Perez, J. M., Gonzalez, P. M., Comi, M. L., & Nieto, C., eds. (2007), *New Developments in Autism: The Future is Today*, London & Philadelphia: Jessica Kingsley Publishers.

Peretz, I. (2009), "Music, language and modularity framed action," *Psychologica Belgica* 49(2–3): 157–75.

Peretz, I., & Coltheart, M. (2003), "Modularity of music processing," *Nature Neuroscience* 6(7): 688–91.

Portmann, A. (1956), *Biologie und Geist*, Zurich: Rhein-Verlag AG.

Pressing, J. (1982), "Pitch Class Set Structures in Contemporary Jazz," *JazzForschung/JazzResearch* 14: 133–72.

Pressing, J. (1984), "Cognitive Processes in Improvisation," in W. Ray Crozier & A. J. Chapman, eds., *Cognitive Processes in the Perception of Art*, Amsterdam: Elsevier.

Pressing, J. (1988), "Improvisation: Methods and Models," in J. A. Sloboda, ed., *Generative Processes in Music*, Oxford: Clarendon.

Randel, D. M., ed. (2003), *The Harvard Dictionary of Music*, 4th ed., Cambridge, MA & London: Harvard University Press.

Rauschecker, J. P. (2006), "Cortical Plasticity and Music," *Annals of the New York Academy of Sciences* 930: 330–36.

Rosch, E. (1975), "Cognitive Reference Points," *Cognitive Psychology* 7: 532–47.

Rose, F. C., ed. (2010), *The Neurology of Music*, London: Imperial College Press.

Rosenboom, D. (2000), *Propositional music: on emergent properties in morphogenesis and the evolution of music*, New York: Granary Books.

Ryle, G. (1949), *The Concept of Mind*, London: Hutchinson's Mayflower Press.

Sawyer, K. (1992), "Improvisational Creativity: An analysis of Jazz Performance," *Creative Research Journal* 5(3): 253–63.

Särkämö, T., Tervaniemi, M., Laitinen, S., Forsblom, Soinila, S., Mikkinen, M., Autti, T., Silvennoinen, H. M., Erkkilä, J., Laine, M., Peretz, I., & Hietanan, M., (2008), "Music listening enhances cognitive recovery and mood after middle cerebral artery stroke," *Brain* 131: 866–76.

Schellenberg, G. (2006), "Music education and intelligence in children," *Psychological Bulletin* 12(2): 893–902.

Schenker, H. (1935), *Der freie Satz*, Vienna: Universal Edition.

Schlaug, G., Jancke, L., Huang, Y., Staiger, J. F., & Steinmetz, H. (1995a), "Increased corpus callosum size in musicians," *Neuropsychologia* 33: 1047–55.

Schlaug, G., Jancke, L., Huang, Y., & Steinmetz, H. (1995b), "In vivo evidence of structural brain asymmetry in musicians," *Science* 267: 699–701.

Schlaug, G., Forgeard, M., Zhou, L., Norton, A., Norton, A. & Winner, E. (2009), "Training-induced neuroplasticity in young children," *Annals of the New York Academy of Science* 1169: 205–08.

Schmitt, L. I., Wimmer, R. D., Nakajama, M., Happ, M., Mofakham, S., & Halaasa, M. (2017), "Thalamic amplification of cortical connectivity sustains attentional control," *Nature* 545: 219–23.

Schneider, D., et al. (2017), "Neural development in a digital age," *Frontiers in Neuroscience* 5: 255–64

Seddon, F. A. (2005), "Modes of Communication during Jazz Improvisation," *British Journal of Music Education* 22(1): 47–61; London: Cambridge University Press.

Shapiro, J., Rucker, L. & Beck, J. (2006), "Training the clinical eye and mind: using the arts to develop medical students' observational and pattern recognition skills," *Medical Education* 40(3): 263–68.

Sherman, S. M., & Guillery, R. W. (2006), *Exploring the Thalamus and its Role in Cortical Functions*, Cambridge, MA: MIT Press.

Sherman, S. M., & Guillery, R. W. (2013), *Functional Connection of Cortical Areas: A New View from the Thalamus*, Cambridge, MA: MIT Press.

Sherman, S. M. (2016), "Thalamus plays a central role in ongoing cortical functioning," *Nature Neuroscience* 19: 533–41.

Simpson, D. (2005), "Phrenology and the Neurosciences: Contributions of F. J. Gall and J. G. Spurzheim," *ANZ Journal of Surgery* 75(6): 3456–65.

Slevc, L. R., & Okada, B. M. (2015), "Processing structure in language and music: a case for shared reliance on cognitive control," *Psychonomic Bulletin and Review* 22(3): 637–52.

Sloboda, J. A. (1985), *The Musical Mind: The Cognitive Psychology of Music*, Oxford: Clarendon Press.

Strait, D. L., & Kraus, N. (2011), "Playing Music for a Smarter Ear: Cognitive, Perceptual and Neurobiological Evidence," *Music Perception* 29(2): 133–46.

Strait, D. L., Chan, K., Ashley, R., & Kraus, N. (2012), "Specialization among the specialized: auditory brainstem function is tuned in to timbre," *Cortex* 48: 360–62.

Stuckey, H. L., & Nobel, J. (2009), "The Connection between art, healing and public health: a review of current literature," *American Journal of Public Health* 100(2): 254–63.

Smith, E. E. (2000), "Neural Bases of Human Working Memory," open access article, *American Psychological Society*.

Smith, G. E. (1991), "In the quest of a new perspective on improvised jazz," *World of Music* 33(3): 29–52.

Southern, E. (1997), *The Music of Black Americans: A History*, 3rd ed., New York & London: W.W. Norton & Company.

Sudnow, D. (1993), *Ways of the Hand*, Cambridge: MIT Press.

Span, L. C., van Dokkum, N. H., Ravensbergen, A. G., Bos, A. F., & Jaschke, A. C. (2021), "Combining kangaroo care and live-performed music therapy: effects on physiological stability and neurological functioning in extremely and very preterm infants," *International Journal of Environmental Research and Public Health* 18(12): 6580.

Thaut, M. (2005), *Rhythm, Music and the Brain: Scientific Foundations and Clinical Appliances*, New York & London: Routledge.

Tillmann, B., Bharucha, J. J., & Bigand, E. (2000), "Implicit learning of tonality: a self-organizing approach," *Psychological Review*, 107: 885–913.

Trepel, M. (2008), *Neuroanatomie, Struktur und Funktion*, München: Urban und Fischer Verlag.

Tomlinson, J. (2015), *A Million Years of Music*, London: Oxford Press.

van Dokkum, N. H., Jaschke, A. C., Ravensbergen, A. G., Reijneveld, S. A., Hakvoort, L., de Kroon, M. A., & Bos, A. F. (2020), "Feasibility of live-performed music therapy for extremely and very preterm infants in a tertiary NICU," *Frontiers in Pediatrics* 8: 581372.

van Dokkum, N. H., Kooi, E. M. W., Berhane, B., Ravensbergen, A. G., Hakvoort, L., Jaschke, A. C., & Bos, A. F. (2021), "Neonatal music therapy and cerebral oxygenation in extremely and very preterm infants: a pilot study," *Music and Medicine, Special Issue* 13(2).

Verhelst, H., & Vander Linden, C. (2016), "Neuroplastic effects of a new multidimensional cognitive training programme in brain-injured adolescents: possible far transfer effects," *Brain Injury* 30(5–6): 601–02.

Vosloo, R. (2010), interview conducted on 23 May 2010.

Wan, C. Y., & Schlaug, G. (2010), "Music making as a tool for promoting brain plasticity across the life span," *Neuroscientist* 16(5): 566–77.

Wan, C. Y. & Schlaug, G. (2010), "Neural pathways for language in autism: potential for music-based treatments," *Future Neurology* 5(6): 797–805.

Wang, Y., Celebrini, S., Trotter, Y., & Barone, P. (2008), Visuo-auditory interactions in the primary visual cortex of the behaving rhesus monkey: electrophysiological evidence," *BMC Neuroscience* 9(79), PMC free article: PMC2527609.

Weisberg, R. W. (2020), *Rethinking Creativity: Inside-the-Box Thinking as the Basis for Innovation*, Cambridge: Cambridge University Press.

Werger, C., Groothuis, M., & Jaschke, A. C. (2020), "Music-based therapeutic interventions 1.0 from music therapy to integrated music technology: a narrative review," *Music and Medicine* 12(2).

WHO (2023), "152 million babies born preterm in the last decade." https://www.who.int/news/item/09-05-2023-152-million-babies-born-preterm-in-the-last-decade. Accessed 05/06/2023.

Wiggins, G. A., Muellensiefen, D., & Pearce, M. T. (2010), "On the nonexistence of music: why music theory is a figment of the imagination," *Musicae Scientiae*, Discussion Forum 5.

Wiesendanger, M. (2010), "Temporal co-ordination of the two hands in playing the violin," in F. C. Rose, ed., *The Neurology of Music*, London: Imperial College Press.

Wolfram, S. (2002), *A New Kind of Science*, Champaigne: Wolfram Media Publishers.

Zatore, R. J., & Salimpoor V. N. (2013), "From perception to pleasure: music and its neural substrates," *Proceedings of the National Academy of Science* 110(2).

Zatorre, R. J., Salimpoor, V. N., Larcher, K., Dagher, A., Benovoy, M. (2011), "Anatomically distinct dopamine release during anticipation and experience of peak emotion to music," *Nature American Neuroscience* 1(11).

Zbikowski, L. (2002), *Conceptualizing Music: Cognitive Structure, Theory and Analysis*, New York: Oxford University Press.

DISCOGRAPHY

Artist, year, *song* < album, LABEL

John Coltrane Quartet, 1964, *Bessie's Blues* < Crescent, IMPULSE!

Nirali Kartik, 2021, *Romantic Maru Bihag – Jaagu Main Sari Raina*
< Navyaa, NIRALI KARTIK

Ales Barta, 2012, *Toccata and Fugue in D Minor, bwv 565*
< Bach: Toccata und Fuge d-Moll, ARCODIVA

Rura, 2018, *I'll Never Forget* < In Praise of Home, RURA MUSIC

Kasír, 2006, *Moonrise* < Reel Irish, GO FOLK MUSIC

Skolvan, 2013, *Trip to Skye* < Entrez dans la danse (Kerzh Ba'n' Dans
– Come to the dance – Breton Music – Celtic Music from Brittany
– Keltia Musique), KELTICA MUSIQUE

Benedictine Monks of Silos, 2008, *Ave Maris Stella* < Gregorian Chant:
The Definitive Collection, JADE/MILAN RECORDS

Göksel Baktagir, Ceyhun Çelikten, Baki Kemancı, 2004,
Gül Bahçesi < Hayal Gibi 2 – Hatira Defteri, YENIKAPI MÜZIK

Sean Jones, 2006, *What We Have* < Roots, MACK AVENUE RECORDS

Miles Davis, 1970, *Bitches Brew (feat. John McLaughlin, Wayne Shorter,
Chick Corea & Joe Zawinul)* < Bitches Brew, COLUMBIA/LEGACY,
DOWNTOWN MUSIC PUBLISHINIG

John Coltrane, 1966, *Ascension – Edition 1 / Pt. 1* < Ascension, VERVE

Miles Davis, 1959, *Blue in Green (feat. John Coltrane & Bill Evans)*
< Kind Of Blue, COLUMBIA/LEGACY, DOWNTOWN MUSIC PUBLISHINIG

Igor Stravinsky, Teodor Currentzis, musicAeterna, 2015, *The Rite of
Spring: Part One: Adoration of the Earth: Dance of the Earth* < Stravinsky:
Le Sacre du Printemps, SONY CLASSICAL

André Rieu, Johann Strauss Orchestra, 2016, *Strauss & Co. Medley*
 < Magic Of The Waltz, POLYDOR

Charles Mingus, 1957, *Haitian Fight Song* < The Clown, RHINO ATLANTIC

Jazz At Lincoln Center Orchestra, Wynton Marsalis, 2020, *Yes or No*
 < The Music of Wayne Shorter, BLUE ENGINE RECORDS

Frédéric Chopin, Simon DuBoise, 2017, *Nocturne #20 in C# Minor P 1*
 No. 16 < Complete Chopin Noctures, ELEMENTS OF DAWN

Guns N' Roses, 1988, *Patience* < G N' R Lies, GEFFEN

Beyoncé, 2003, *Me, Myself and I* < Dangerously In Love, COLUMBIA

Gustav Mahler, Concertgebouworkest, Mariss Jansons, 2010,
 Mahler: Symphony No 2 in c Minor, "Resurrection": iv. Urlicht
 – Live < Mahler: Symphony No. 2, "Resurrection" (Live),
 ROYAL CONCERTGEBOUW ORCHESTRA

Eminem, 2004, *Like Toy Soldiers* < Encore (Deluxe Version), AFTERMATH

2Pac, 2004, *Ghetto Gospel* < Loyal To The Game, AMARU

Hans Zimmer, 2003, *A Hard Teacher* < The Last Samurai:
 Original Motion Picture Score, ELEKTRA RECORDS

Rachel Portman, 2008, *The Duchess* < The Duchess Music from
 the Motion Picture, LAKESHORE RECORDS

Various Artists, 1993, *I Got You Babe* < Groundhog Day: Music From
 The Original Motion Picture Soundtrack, EPIC SOUNDTRAX

John Williams, 1980, *Yoda's Theme* < Star Wars: The Empire Strikes Back
 (Original Motion Picture Soundtrack), WALT DISNEY RECORDS

Nostalgia 77, 2007, *Quiet Dawn* < Everything Under the Sun, TRU THOUGHTS

Dream Theater, 2002, *The Great Debate* < Six Degrees of Inner
 Turbulence, ATLANTIC RECORDS

André Hazes, 1981, *Zeg Maar Niets Meer* < Gewoon André, N/A

Dmitri Shostakovich, Eder Quartet, 1994, *String Quartet No. 4*
 in D Major, Op. 83: IV. Allegretto < Shostakovich: String Quartets
 Nos. 4, 6 and 7, NAXOS

John Cage, Stephen Drury, 1994, *Music for Marcel Duchamp (1947)*
 < In a Landscape: Piano Music of John Cage, CATALYST

Various Artists, 1985, *Der Kleine Leutnant Des Lieben Gottes*
(*The Little Lieutenant of the Loving God*) < Lost In The Stars:
The Music Of Kurt Weill, A&M

Karlheinz Stockhausen, Ensemble C.L.S.I., Paul Méfano, 2018,
*Kurzwellen, Work No. 25, System 1: Second W Radio Solo Followed
by Instrumental quartet [2 Synchronous Events]* < Stockhausen:
Kurzwellen, MODE RECORDS

**Richard Wagner, Siegfried Jerusalem, Daniel Barenboim,
Berliner Philharmoniker**, 1996, *Wagner: Tristan und Isolde: Prelude to Act 1*
< Wagner: Tristan und Isolde, WARNER CALSSICS INTERNATIONAL

Ludwig van Beethoven, Fazıl Say, 2014, *Piano Sonata No. 14 in c-Sharp
Minor, Op. 27 No. 2 "Moonlight": 1. Adagio sostenuto* < Beethoven:
Concerto et Sonates, NAÏVE CLASSIQUE

The Beatles, 1996, *The End – Anthology 3 Version* < Anthology 3, EMI

Black Sabbath, 1970, *War Pigs* < Paranoid, VERTIGO

Def Leppard, 1980 < *On through the Night*, VERTIGO

Godspeed You! Black Emperor, 1997, *Dead flag Blues* < F# A# ∞,
CONSTELLATION – KRANKY

ABOUT THE AUTHOR

Dr. Artur C. Jaschke studied double-bass and drums at Dartington College of Arts. He holds a PhD in clinical Neuropsychology from the VU University Amsterdam. He is Lector in Music-Based Therapies and Interventions and in Ecologies of Clinical Neuromusicology: Creative AI , Music Sciences and Health Care Applications at the department of Music Therapy at ArtEZ University of the Arts (NL), as well as senior clinical Research Fellow of Cognitive Neuroscience of Music at the Neonatal Intensive Care Unit of the University Medical Center Groningen and the Cambridge Institute for Music Therapy Research (UK). Furthermore, he is Research Associate at the Department of Psychiatry at the University of Cambridge (UK).

ABOUT SUKHDEV SANDUH

Sukhdev Sandhu is the Director of the Center for Experimental Humanities and an Associate Professor of English Literature and Social and Cultural Analysis at New York University. He is also the author of, among others, *London Calling: How Black and Asian Writers Imagined a City* and *I'll Get My Coat*. His writings have appeared in a number of publications including the *London Review of Books, Suddeutsche Zeitung, The Guardian, Times Literary Supplement*. He makes radio documentaries for the BBC, runs the Colloquium for Unpopular Culture at New York University, and is a film critic.

ABOUT THE PUBLISHERS

The New Menard Press is the British imprint of HetMoet
Publishing, an indie press based on a historic sailing barge in
Amsterdam, the Netherlands, and was founded by Elte Rauch in
2018. The former Menard Press was founded by Anthony Rudolf
in 1969.

Please get in touch at info@thenewmenardpress.com
Subscribe to our newsletter, visit: www.thenewmenardpress.com

Follow us on:
[instagram] @thenew_menardpress
[facebook] TheNewMenardPress

Mind the Music: On Improvisation, Music and the Brain
Artur Christoph Jaschke

This edition was first published in the United Kingdom in February 2024
by The New Menard Press (www.thenewmenardpress.com)

ISBN 9789083206097

Text editing by Penny Iremonger
Typeset in Plantin MT and Gotham
Book design by Armée de Verre Bookdesign, Ghent, Belgium
Printed and bound Patria, The Netherlands
Distribution and sales: Booksource, Glasgow (orders@booksource.net)
InPress Ltd Newcastle upon Tyne
www.inpressbooks.co.uk

This edition was supported by the Professorship Music-based Therapies and
Interventions at ArtEZ University of the Arts.